PENGUIN BOOKS — GREAT FOOD

From Absinthe to Zest

Author of *The Count of Monte Cristo* and *The Three Musketeers*, ALEXANDRE DUMAS (1802–1870) was a prolific writer who also wrote plays, short stories, essays, magazine articles and reportage. In addition to this he was an expert cook and great traveller, whose cosmopolitan outlook is reflected in *The Great Dictionary of Cuisine*, first published posthumously in 1873. An encyclopedia running from 'Absinthe' to 'Zest', collecting culinary terms, recipes and anecdotes, Dumas wrote *The Dictionary* 'to be read by the sophisticated and used by the practitioners of the art'.

From Absinthe to Zest

An Alphabet for Food Lovers

ALEXANDRE DUMAS

PENGUIN BOOKS

PENGUIN BOOKS

Published by the Penguin Group
Penguin Group (USA) Inc., 375 Hudson Street, New York, New York 10014, USA
Penguin Group (Canada), 90 Eglinton Avenue East, Suite 700, Toronto, Ontario,
Canada M4P 2Y3 (a division of Pearson Penguin Canada Inc.)
Penguin Books Ltd, 80 Strand, London WC2R 0RL, England
Penguin Ireland, 25 St. Stephen's Green, Dublin 2, Ireland
(a division of Penguin Books Ltd)
Penguin Books Australia Ltd, 250 Camberwell Road, Camberwell, Victoria 3124,
Australia (a division of Pearson Australia Group Pty Ltd)
Penguin Books India Pvt Ltd, 11 Community Centre, Panchsheel Park,
New Delhi – 110 017, India
Penguin Group (NZ), 67 Apollo Drive, Rosedale, Auckland 0632, New Zealand
(a division of Pearson New Zealand Ltd)
Penguin Books (South Africa) (Pty) Ltd, 24 Sturdee Avenue,
Rosebank, Johannesburg 2196, South Africa

Penguin Books Ltd, Registered Offices: 80 Strand, London WC2R 0RL, England

Le Grand Dictionnaire de Cuisine first published in France 1873
Abridged translation published in Great Britain as *Dumas on Food* by Michael Joseph 1978
This extract first published in Great Britain in Penguin Books 2011
First published in the USA by Viking Studio, a member of Penguin Group
(USA) Inc. 2011
1 3 5 7 9 10 8 6 4 2

Translation copyright © Alan and Jane Davidson, 1978
All rights reserved

Printed in Great Britain by Clays Ltd, St Ives plc

Cover design based on a pattern from a dish by Jules-Louis Pull, *c.* 1890.
Earthenware with inlaid decoration. (Photograph copyright © Victoria & Albert
Museum.) Picture research by Samantha Johnson. Lettering by Stephen Raw.

ISBN: 978–0–241–95637–3

www.penguin.com

Contents

One More Word to the Public

After I had decided to write this book and to crown with it, so to speak, in a time of relaxation, my literary work of four or five hundred volumes, I found myself, I admit, quite perplexed; not about its substance, but about the form to be given to the work.

Whatever my approach to it, people would expect of me more than I could give.

If I made of it a book of imagination and wit, like the *Physiologie du Goût* of Brillat-Savarin, the professionals, the cooks of both sexes, would pay no attention to me.

If I made of it a practical work, like the *Cuisinière bourgeoise*, the more sophisticated people would say: 'It would have been just about as useless for Michelet to tell him [Dumas] that he was the most skilful dramatist since Shakespeare, or for Ourliac to tell him that he possessed not only the French spirit but also that of Gascony, as for Dumas to come and teach us in a book of eight hundred pages how to skin rabbits and hares.'

This was not my aim. I wanted my book to be read by the sophisticated and used by the practitioners of the art.

At the beginning of the century Grimod de la Reynière had some success in publishing *l'Almanach des Gourmands*; but this was a straightforward book of gastronomy, not a book of recipes.

What especially tempted me, the indefatigable traveller who had voyaged through Italy and Spain, countries where one eats poorly, and through the Caucasus and Africa, countries where one does not eat at all, was to indicate all the ways of eating better in the former category of countries and of eating somehow or other in the latter category; granted that to achieve this result one would have to be prepared to do one's own hunting and foraging.

Here is the formula on which, after a lengthy deliberation with myself, I settled. To take from the classic cookery books which had passed into the public domain, such as the dictionary of the author of the *Mémoires de Mme de Créqui*, from the *Art du Cuisinier* of Beauvilliers, the most recent expert, from le père Durand of Nîmes, from the great collections of the epoch of Louis XIV and Louis XV, all the culinary recipes which have won citizens' rights at the best tables. To borrow from Carême, that apostle of the gastronomes, what Messieurs Garnier, his editors, would let me take. To take another look at the witty writings of the marquis de Cussy, and to appropriate for myself his best inventions. To re-read Elzéar-Blaz and, uniting my hunting instincts with his, to try to devise something new on the cookery of quails and ortolans. To add to all this some dishes which are unknown [here], gathered from all the countries of the world, with the most original and witty anecdotes about the cuisines of other peoples and about these peoples themselves. And finally, to deal with the physiology of all the animals and plants which are edible and which are worth describing.

In this way my book, containing both scientific knowledge and an element of wit, would not seem too daunting to the practitioners and would also perhaps deserve to be read by men of serious character – and even by women of a much lighter disposition, who would not fear that their fingers would grow weary in turning my pages, some of which resemble those of M. de Maistre [a notoriously boring writer] and others those of Sterne [the novelist].

This established, I begin, quite naturally, with the letter A.

P.S. Let me not forget to say, for such an omission would be an act of ingratitude, that I have consulted separately, for certain recipes, the great restaurateurs of Paris and even those in the provinces; such as the proprietor of the café Anglais, Verdier, Brébant, Magny, les Frères-Provençaux, Pascal, Grignon, Peter's, Véfour, Véry and, above all, my old friend Vuillemot.

Wherever they have had the kindness to place their knowledge at my disposition, there you will find their names. Let them receive here my thanks.

A.D.
(Alexandre Dumas)

Dictionary from A–Z

ABSINTHE (or WORMWOOD)   *ABSINTHE*

This perennial has very bitter leaves. It is to be found throughout Europe; and in the north a wine called vermouth is made from it.

There are two kinds of absinthe, the great absinthe called Roman, and the small kind called Pontic or Little absinthe. The plant is also known under the name Marine absinthe. Both sorts, from the seaside and from the mountains, are eaten with pleasure. It is to the latter especially that the flavour of those animals whose meat is so esteemed by gourmands as *pré-salé* is due.

Even though all the old recipe collections vaunt absinthe as a tonic for the stomach and an aid to digestion, and even though the Salerno school recommends it as a preventative against seasickness, it is impossible not to deplore the ravages which absinthe has wrought over the past forty years among our soldiers and our poets. There is not a single regimental surgeon who will not say that absinthe has killed more Frenchmen in Africa than the *flitta*, the *yatagan* [Arab weapons] or the Arab gun.

Some of our bohemian poets have called absinthe the green Muse. Some others, not in this group, have died from the poisonous embraces of this same Muse. Hégesippe Moreau, Amédée Roland and Alfred de Musset,

our greatest poet after Hugo and Lamartine, all suc-
cumbed to the disastrous effect of this liqueur.

The fatal passion of de Musset for absinthe, which
perhaps served also to give his verses such a bitter flavour, caused the sober Academy to fall into the near
likeness of a pun. The fact was that de Musset missed
many sessions of the Academy, finding himself not in a
fit state to attend.

'In truth,' said M. Villemain, one of the Forty, 'do you
not find that Alfred de Musset is *absent* a little too frequently?'

'You mean to say that he *absinthes* himself too much.'

ANCHOVY   *ANCHOIS*

A sea fish, smaller than a finger, with no scales. [Dumas
was misinformed. The anchovy has scales. But they come
off at the slightest handling, so that when the fish reach
the consumer they may well have none.] The anchovy
has a big head, large black eyes, a very big mouth, a sil-
very body and a rounded back. It is found in abundance
on the Provençal coast, and it is from there that it comes
to us as *anchois confits* or as anchovies in a marinade.

The flesh of the anchovy has a delicate flavour. It may
be grilled, and it is easy to digest. It may also be cured
with vinegar and salt, which form a brine in which it is
preserved. Preserved anchovy only appears on our tables
as an hors d'oeuvre, or is used simply as a seasoning. It
has, from its nature and from the way in which it is prepared, a stimulating quality which facilitates digestion
when it is used in moderation.

Rôties d'anchois • Anchovy toasts
Fry long, thin slices of bread in oil, arrange them on a platter and pour over them a sauce made of virgin oil, lemon juice, coarsely ground pepper, parsley, spring onion and chopped Spanish garlic [*rocambole*, but ordinary garlic will do]. Half cover the slices of fried bread with anchovy fillets which you have dipped in white wine.

ANISE   *ANISE*

An aromatic plant belonging to the family of umbelliferous plants; it is abundant throughout Europe, in Egypt and in Syria, in Italy and above all in Rome. It is the despair of foreigners who cannot escape from its taste or smell. It is put in pastries and in bread; and the Neapolitans put it in everything. In Germany it is the main seasoning of that bread which one finds accompanying figs and dried pears, and which has retained the name of *pompernick* (pumpernickel). This comes from the exclamation of a certain horseman who, having tasted one mouthful, immediately took the rest to his horse, which was called Nick, saying '*Bon pour Nick*', which with the German accent is *Pompernick*.

APRICOT   *ABRICOT*

The tree which bears this fruit came to the Romans from Armenia; so they called it *prunus armeniaca*. To begin with, only two species of apricot were known, but a number of varieties have been obtained.

It is a fruit containing a nut. Its skin and flesh are tinged with the colour of chamois. It has a pleasant smell and a good taste, bearing some resemblance to the peach and the plum; and is such an early fruit that there are few springs when one does not hear people saying: 'There will be no apricots this year, they've all been caught by the frost.'

Apart from the various kinds of apricot which we gather in France, Chardin, during his voyage in Persia, ate excellent apricots which had red flesh and a delicious flavour. These are called *tocmchams*, meaning 'eggs of the sun'. It is at Damascus in Syria that one eats the best apricots. The people there make excellent apricot jams and cakes.

[Dumas proceeds to refer to a kind of apricot grown in Santo Domingo, his father's birthplace. In a footnote of a kind which occurs but rarely in his Dictionary, he says that he has taken the details from the *Dictionnaire des Aliments et des Boissons*, by M. Aulagnier, and implies that he has used this as a source of information about fruits all over the world, but especially in the French colonies.]

By means of this excellent fruit a delicious scent is given to sorbets and ices. It provides material for excellent cakes, fritters, tarts, flans, creams and conserves.

Tourte ou Gateau fourré d'abricots à la bonne femme •
A 'tart' or 'cake' filled with apricots
Split and peel the apricots, cook them with a little sugar and let the resulting compote cool.

Arrange the half apricots on a layer of puff pastry,

then cover them with a second layer of puff pastry. This upper layer should be slashed or pricked, so that it will not swell up and assume a crooked shape during the cooking. Brush the top and edges with egg-yolk, so that they will take on a golden colour, and cook the *tourte* in a *four de campagne*.

Mixing some cherries with the apricots produces an excellent effect, and this modern combination has been generally adopted in the leading kitchens of Paris.

Compote d'abricots à la minute •

A quickly made compote of apricots
Make a syrup [of sugar] and, once it is thick enough, boil in it your apricots, split in half. After three minutes, skim the compote, add the juice of an orange and let it cool.

BEANS   *HARICOTS*

Beans are eaten in three ways, and at three different stages of their development Before they are fully grown, they are eaten with their seeds, and are then called green beans. Just before they are fully mature, the seeds, which are still tender, are eaten; and they are then called flageo-lets. Finally, they are much eaten in dried form, and are then known, irrespective of where they come from, as beans from Soissons.

As I come from the *département* of Aisne, it is up to me to assert the worth of my compatriots and, until my last trip to Asia, I had always declared that Soissons beans were the best in the world. But I have now been forced to acknowledge the superiority of the beans from Trebizond.

But, whether from Trebizond or Soissons, dried beans have one serious disadvantage. There are some waters in which they refuse to cook. Science must then battle against nature. In this case, prepare a little cloth bag, knotted together and containing new wood ash, and put it in the cooking water; or, better still, a little bicarbonate of soda. Even the most refractory bean will be defeated by this treatment.

BEAR   *OURS*

There are few people of our generation who do not recall the sensation caused by the first instalment of my *Impressions de Voyage* when people read the article entitled 'Bear steak'. There was a universal outcry against the audacious narrator who dared to say that there were places in civilized Europe where bear is eaten.

It would have been easier to go to Chevet, and ask him if he had bear hams.

He would have enquired without a trace of surprise: 'Is it a Canadian leg or one from Transylvania which you wish?' And he would have furnished whichever he was asked for.

I could at that time have given to readers the advice which I give them today, but I took good care not to; there was a big commotion about the book, and since at that time I was just embarking on a literary career I could ask for nothing better.

But to my great astonishment, the person who should

have been most pleased by the uproar, the innkeeper, de Martigny, was furious; he wrote me to upbraid me, he wrote to the newspapers to get them to state in his name that he had never served bear to his travellers; but his fury kept increasing as each traveller asked him as their first question: 'Do you have any bear?'

If the stupid man had thought to answer yes, and then served ass, horsemeat or mule instead of bear, he would have made a fortune.

Since that time we have become more civilized; bear hams have become a dish which one doesn't meet in every salted-provision dealer's premises, but which one can find without too much difficulty.

The brown bear is commonly found in the Alps; the grey bear, the most implacable of all, who first puts the horse to flight and then its rider, is to be found in America. There are in Canada and in Savoy reddish bears who don't eat meat, but who are so partial to honey and milk that they would rather be killed than let go when they are holding a honeycomb or a jug of milk. Black bears only live in cold countries. The forests and countryside of Kamtschatka are full of bears who only attack when they are attacked themselves; and a peculiar thing is that they never harm women, whom they nevertheless follow, to steal the fruit which they are gathering.

When the Yakuts, a Siberian people, meet a bear, they doff their caps, greet him, call him master, old man or grandfather, and promise not to attack him or even to speak ill of him. But if he looks as though he may pounce on them, they shoot at him and, if they kill him, they cut him in pieces and roast him and regale themselves, repeating all the while: 'It is the Russians who are eating you, not us.' (A-F. Aulagnier, *Dictionnaire des Aliments et des Boissons*.)

Bear meat is now eaten by all the peoples of Europe. Since ancient times, the front feet have been regarded as the best part of the animal. The Chinese have a high regard for them, and in Germany, where meat from the bear cub is greatly enjoyed, the front feet are a delicacy for rich people.

Here, according to M. Urbain Dubois, the cook of Their Majesties of Prussia, is the way in which these feet are served in Moscow, Saint Petersburg and throughout all of Russia. The paws are sold skinned. One starts by washing them, salting them, putting them in a terrine and covering them with a marinade cooked with vinegar, in which they are allowed to steep for two or three days.

Then line a casserole with bacon and ham trimmings and chopped vegetables. Lay the bear's feet on the vegetables, cover them with the marinade, some bouillon and some bards of bacon; let them cook for seven or eight hours on a very low flame, adding liquid as it reduces.

When the paws are cooked, leave them in the liquid until they are nearly cold. They should then be drained and wiped, divided lengthwise in four, sprinkled with cayenne pepper and rolled in melted lard. Roll them in breadcrumbs and grill them gently for half an hour. Then arrange them on a platter into which you have poured a piquant sauce (reduced, with two spoonfuls of currant jelly added as a finishing touch).

BOAR   *SANGLIER*

This is pig in its wild state; and hunting it is not without
danger. The boar is quite a misanthropic animal, which
on reaching a certain age seeks refuge in the thickest
brambles and thickets, where it does not like to be dis-
turbed. At this time it takes the name of *ragot* (two-year-
old boar), *quartanier* (four-year-old boar) and *solitaire*
(boar of advanced age). It is rare that one of these animals, armed as it is with redoubtable defences, does not
turn on the hunter who has shot at him. The best the
hunter can do then, if there is the branch of a tree within
reach, is to hang from it until the boar has passed, for it
rarely attacks the same target twice. I have retailed stories about several of the hunts of my youth, which were
not without some very original anecdotes on just this
point.

Young boar are skinned, and are eaten spit-roasted.

The forequarters, the head and the fillets are the best
parts of the boar. Likewise, chops similar to pork chops
are cut. However, since the boar is difficult to bleed one
cannot always collect the blood in order to make *boudin*
of it.

Quartier de sanglier à la royale ·
                  Quarter of wild boar *à la royale*
Skin and singe a quarter of a wild sow, bone it up to the
knuckle and lard it with spices and aromatics, previously pounded. Put it in a terrine with a lot of salt,
pepper, juniper, thyme, bay leaf, basil, onions and spring
onions; and let it marinate for five days. When you want

9

to cook it, remove the aromatics which remain within it, wrap it in a white cloth, and tie it up like a joint of beef. Put it in a braising pan with the liquid of its marinade, six bottles of white wine, the same amount of water, six carrots, six onions, four cloves, a good bouquet of parsley and spring onions, and salt if there is not enough. Let it barely simmer for six hours. Try it, to see whether it has cooked sufficiently; otherwise give it another hour. Let it rest in the cooking liquid for half an hour and, when you remove it, leave the rind on.

CAKE   *GÂTEAU*

Cakes, a sort of pastry, are almost always round in shape, and usually made with flour, eggs and butter. They can also be made of rice. Their name (*gâteau*) without doubt comes from the prodigality with which children are spoiled (*gâtés*) by having cakes given to them either as a reward, or as an encouragement of a gastronomic nature.

The most famous of all the cakes is the *gâteau des Rois* (Twelfth Night cake), a sort of broad thin cake in which a broad bean is placed. This ancient patriarchal custom has become universal, and there are few families who do not choose to have a reunion at Epiphany, and distribute sections of the *gâteau des rois*.

In certain provinces, aside from the parts to be taken by those present, a portion for God in his charity is also cut. This is given to the first beggar who passes by, and consequently becomes the portion of poverty.

Everyone knows that it is the youngest person present who is in charge of serving and distributing the slices of cake. For Barjac, the manservant of Cardinal de Fleury, it was the occasion for a bit of light-hearted flattery.

On one Twelfth Night, he managed to assemble at his master's table twelve guests of such advanced age that, even though His Eminence was already well over ninety, he was still the youngest person present and had to fulfil the tasks which are usually allocated to the children; a happening which gave him a most agreeable surprise.

Now, here are a few recipes:

Gâteau à la Madeleine • Madeleine cake

Break ten eggs, separating the yolks from the whites. Beat the yolks with three *quarterons* (367 grams) of powdered sugar, a pinch of chopped green lemon, and a little fine salt. Add half a *livre* (245 grams) best quality flour, and mix everything together well. Incorporate a good-sized piece of best quality clarified butter in this mixture, add six well-beaten egg whites, and finish off your batter. Next, butter some little Madeleine moulds, fill them with this mixture, bake them at a low temperature, then serve them.

You can substitute for the little moulds a large baking tray covered with buttered paper, on to which you put the batter. You then cook the cake, and cut it into lozenge shapes, or whatever other shapes you like.

Gâteau au fromage de Brie •
Cake made with Brie cheese

Take some fine Brie cheese, knead it with a litre of flour, 90 grams of butter and a little salt. Add five or six eggs and thin the dough well, working it with the palm of

11

your hand. Next, let it rest for half an hour; then roll it out with a rolling pin. Shape the cake in the usual way, brush it with egg, put it in the oven to cook, and serve.

Cake; ou Kake (gâteau anglais) ·

English wedding cake

The practice in England, as we can read in the works of Dickens, is to make an enormous cake on the occasion of the wedding of one's offspring and to distribute a slice of this to each guest.

This is how the cake is made. Take 2 kilos of good quality flour, 2 kilos of fresh butter, a kilo of finely sieved sugar and 7 grams of nutmeg. For each pound of flour eight eggs are required. Wash and pick over 2 kilos of currants which you dry in front of the fire. Take 500 grams of sweet almonds, which must be blanched, skinned and cut into slivers; add to these 500 grams of candied lemon peel, 500 grams of candied orange peel and half a litre of brandy.

Work the butter with your hands, and then beat it with the sugar for a quarter of an hour. Beat the whites of your eggs, mix with the butter and sugar, then add the flour and nutmeg and beat all together, mixing the currants and almonds in well. Make three layers, alternating them with the lemon and orange peel. Put in a mould and place in the oven, cover with paper and leave until perfectly baked.

Gâteau à l'anglaise · English cake
Mix some flour with some milk and cream, add half a pound of dried chopped raisins, and the same amount

of beef suet, some coriander, grated nutmeg, orange-flower water and brandy. Mix it all well together, butter the base of a casserole, put your cake mixture in and cook it in the oven. At the moment of serving, glaze it with sugar.

CELERY   *CÉLERI*

Celery is the plant with which, in classical times, people would garland themselves during their meals, to neutralize the strong effects of wine. 'Let us fill the goblets with the Massic wine, which causes all ills to be forgotten,' said Horace, 'let us draw their perfumes through these large *pompes* [presumably *pompes de cellier*, which were tubes through which wine-tasters could draw up a taste of wine from a barrel], and may they hurry to make us wreaths of celery and myrtle.'

Salade de céleri
Celery which is full, tender and fresh, seasoned with aromatic vinegar and with oil from Provence and a little good mustard, and then eaten as a salad is really delicious. It awakens the stomach to activity and gives one both an appetite and a sort of alacrity which lasts for several hours.

COCK   *COQ*

The cock is unquestionably the most glorious, most vigilant and most courageous of birds.

As to pride, one has only to watch him parading in

the middle of his harem of hens to recognize that in this respect he rivals the peacock. As to vigilance, he never sleeps more than two hours at a stretch; from one o'clock in the morning, he wrests man from sleep with his piercing cry and sends him back to his work. As for courage, Levaillant reports in his *Mémoires* that his cock was the only one of his animals to remain unperturbed by the approach or roar of a lion.

For a while, during the First Empire, there was some question of taking the ancient cock of the Gauls as emblem and insignia for the French flag. The Emperor Napoleon the First, to whom the proposal was submitted, refused, replying: 'I don't want the cock, because *the fox eats it*.' And he chose the eagle.

In cooking, the cock is used only for making consommé. The ancient recipe collections attributed heroic virtues to this consommé, known under the name of *gelée de coq*.

The virgin cock, the bachelor of the farm-yard, nevertheless owes to its continence and its virtue its particular taste and aroma. These distinguish it clearly from its uncle, the capon, who, as is well known, is not the father but the uncle of chickens. It is eaten after having been simply barded and cooked on a spit, for it would be an outrage to lard it and a dishonour to put it in a stew.

To conclude, the cock is a very handsome animal, gallant, intrepid and endowed with a sonorous voice, and highly representative of the French spirit. But it is worth very little in the kitchen, where its offspring are preferred.

COFFEE   *CAFÉ*

The plant which produces coffee is a very low, small shrub which bears fragrant flowers. Coffee comes originally from the Yemen, in Arabia Felix. At present it is cultivated in several countries. The Arab historian, Ahmet-Effendi, thinks that it was a dervish who discovered coffee, in about the fifteenth century, or in the year 650 of the Hegira.

The first European to refer to the coffee plant was Prosper Alpin, of Padua. In 1580 he accompanied a Venetian consul to Egypt. The work of which we are speaking was written in Latin, and addressed to Jean Morazini.

I have seen this tree in Cairo, in the gardens of Ali Bey. It is called *bon* or *boun*. With the berry which it produces, the Egyptians produce a drink which Arabs call *Kawa*. The taste for coffee grew to such an extent at Constantinople that the Imams complained that the mosques were deserted whereas the cafés were always full. Amurat III then permitted coffee to be consumed in private houses, as long as the doors were shut.

Coffee was unknown in France until 1657, when the Venetians first brought it to Europe. It was introduced to France through Marseilles. It became universally used, and the doctors were alarmed about it. But their sinister predictions were treated as unreal, and the result was that, despite the arguments, the cafés were no less frequented.

In 1669, the Ambassador from Mahomet II brought a large quantity to France and we are assured that coffee was being sold in Paris at that time for up to 40 crowns a pound.

Posée-Oblé, in his *Histoire des plantes de la Guyane*, written during the reign of Louis XIII, says that in Paris, near Petit-Châtelet, the decoction made of coffee and known as *cahuet* was being sold. In 1676, an Armenian named Pascale established at the market of Saint-Germain a café which he later moved to the quai de l'Ecole. He made quite a fortune out of it. But it was only at the beginning of the following century that a Sicilian called Procope re-established the coffee market at Saint-Germain. He attracted the best people in Paris, because he only provided good merchandise. Later, he set up his business in quarters opposite the Comédie Française; this new café became both a rendez-vous for theatre enthusiasts, and a battle-ground for literary disputes. It was in this café that Voltaire spent two hours every day. In London, during the same period, more than three thousand coffee houses were established. Mme de Sevigné fought against the new fashion as hard as she could and predicted that Racine and the café would pass out of fashion simultaneously.

There are five principal sorts of coffee in commerce, without counting chicory, which our cooks are bent on mixing in. The best comes from *Moka* in Arabia Felix, and it alone is also divided into three varieties: *baouri*, which is reserved for the use of the great lords, *saki* and *salabi*.

Coffee from Reunion is highly esteemed in the trade but, even so, that from Martinique or Guadeloupe is preferred. That from Santo Domingo (Dominican Republic), which also includes Puerto Rico and other Islands of the Leeward group, is of inferior quality.

Coffee had come into general usage in France when, in 1808, Napoleon published his decree concerning the 'continental system' [blockade], which was to deprive France of sugar and coffee at the same time. Beet sugar was substituted for cane sugar, and coffee was eked out by mixing it half and half with chicory. This was completely to the advantage of the grocers and cooks who took to chicory with passion and maintained that chicory mixed with coffee tasted better and was healthier. The misfortune is that even today, when the continental decree has fallen into disuse, chicory remains a part of our cooks' repertoire and they have continued mixing a certain quantity of it with the coffee (which they buy ready ground) under the pretext of refreshing their masters. The masters responded to this situation by ordering coffee to be bought in the bean. But, in moulds made especially for this purpose, chicory paste has been made into the shape of coffee beans; and, whether one will or no, chicory has remained wedded to coffee.

It is usual for coffee made with water, and served after a meal, to be accompanied by a small pitcher of milk which has not been boiled, or cream. This can then be added to the coffee if one likes it this way.

DOG   *CHIEN*

Some Asian, African and American peoples eat dog meat. Negroes even prefer it to other animals; their greatest treat is roast dog. This same taste is also to be found among the savages of Canada, in the Kamtchadales and in the islands of Oceania.

Captain Cook was saved from a dangerous illness by dog bouillon. Hippocrates says the Greeks ate dog and that the Romans served it at the most sumptuous tables. Pliny assures us that small dogs, roasted, are excellent, and that they were considered to be worthy offerings to the gods. In Rome, roast dog was always eaten at the feasts given for the consecration of pontiffs or at public celebrations.

Now this is how Porphyrus, the third-century Greek writer, explains the origin of the custom of eating dog.

'One day, when a dog was being sacrificed, a certain part of the victim (they don't say which) fell to the ground. The priest picked it up in order to replace it on the altar, but, as it was very hot, he burnt himself. In a gesture which was natural and spontaneous in the circumstances, he put his fingers in his mouth and found the juices good. Once the ceremony was over, he ate half the dog, and took the rest to his wife. Then, on the occasion of each subsequent sacrifice, he and his wife feasted on the victim. Word of this soon spread all over town; everyone wanted to taste it and in a very short while roast dog was to be found on the best tables. They started by cooking puppies, which naturally were more tender; then, when there were not enough of these, larger dogs were used.'

The official reports of the recent expedition by the English to China have given us some very strange details on the feeding habits of the Chinese. Amongst other things, we learn that they fatten dogs in cages, much as we do chickens. They feed them vegetable matter, then eat them and find them excellent. This is, it seems, one of the most choice dishes in the celestial empire. It is sold by all Chinese butchers, but it is a delicacy which, like our truffled turkeys, is reserved for the fortunate few; and common mortals are obliged to make do with the sight of it only.

DUMPLING   *DUMPLING*

Foreign cooking, an English dessert.

Dumpling aux pommes ou aux prunes •
Apple or plum dumpling
Roll out your hot pastry-dough thin and lay on it peeled apples or plums from Damascus. Having dampened the edges of the dough and closed the edges, boil the whole thing in a cloth for an hour. Pour hot melted butter over it, sprinkle it with sugar and serve.

[We have done our best, with the help of pastry experts on both sides of the Channel, to make sense of this recipe, but have concluded that it can only be presented as an example of how Dumas could go astray in dealing with dishes with which he was not familiar.

An apple dumpling made in England in the nineteenth century would have been made with suet-crust pastry, and would have been wrapped in a cloth, and boiled or steamed (for two hours, not one). But the use of the word *'chaud'* seems to show that Dumas meant hot-water crust pastry (the same as raised pie pastry) to be used. This would have been totally unsuitable for boiling!

A possible explanation of the confusion is that in certain parts of England, e.g. Nottinghamshire and Gloucestershire, fruit pies were made with hot-water crust pastry in the eighteenth and nineteenth centuries. Dumas might have come across such a recipe and somehow amalgamated it in his mind with the recipe for apple dumpling. But this seems rather unlikely.

Dumas' suggestion that plums could be used instead of apples is interesting. It may be the result of his interest in English plum puddings. These, however, do not contain plums.]

Dumpling de Norfolk • Norfolk dumpling
This dish, which owes its name to the Duke of Norfolk, who had a great affection for it, is made in the following way. You add to a fairly thick dough a big glass of milk, two eggs and a little salt. Cook it for two or three minutes in quickly boiling water. Discard the water, drain the dumpling and serve it with slightly salted butter. [Norfolk dumplings are named for the county, not for any Duke thereof. They are not made in the manner described; and if they were, they could not possibly be cooked in 'two or three minutes'. Nor are they served with slightly salted butter. What people in Norfolk and many other English counties used to do was to keep back some of the dough from bread-baking, make large dumplings therewith (say, ¼ lb each), boil them for about fifteen minutes and serve them in the meat gravy. See, for example, Elizabeth David's *English Bread and Yeast Cookery*, Allen Lane, 1977.]

DURIAN   *DURION*

This is the name given to a fruit which grows on a very
tall tree, which is remarkable for its size, and resembles
our melons. The tree comes from India originally, and
the Siamese like the durian so much that they keep it
available, preserved, all year. By cooking it with fresh
cream they make a *marmelade* which they put into
pots.

The durian is enveloped in a skin which is harder
than that of chestnuts, and covered with very sharp
spikes. The smell of the skin is disagreeable and has the
taste of roasted onions, but the flesh of the fruit has an
exquisite taste. In this flesh there is a small nut containing a kernel which people toast and then eat. It tastes
like our chestnuts.

EGGS   *ŒUFS*

An organic body, laid by female birds, which encloses
the growth of a germ. Hens' eggs are those most frequently used for human nourishment.

'It is obvious', says M. Payen, 'that this foodstuff contains all the essential elements for the formation of
animal tissues, since it suffices without any external
nutriment for the evolution of the germ, which little by
little is transformed into a small animal composed of
muscle, tendon, bone, skin, etcetera.'

In fact, one finds in the egg nitrogenous substances,
fats and sugars, sulphur, phosphorus and mineral salts.
The white is formed of albumen.

Eggs are one of the foodstuffs which are most difficult to find fresh in winter. Now, everyone knows that there is no taste more disagreeable than that of an egg which is not fresh. Almost all cookery books advise you to lay in your supply between the two feast days of Our Lady, that is to say between 15 August and mid-September. [The Assumption of Our Lady is celebrated on 15 August and her Nativity on 8 September.] The best way to preserve them then is to bury them in fresh wood ash in which have been mixed branches of juniper, bay and other aromatic woods. It is good to mix some very fine, dry sand into these ashes.

Moreover, there is one very simple way of knowing whether an egg is still good. Place it in a cup full of water. If one of the ends rises, and tends to stay upright, that shows that the egg is one third empty, and consequently inedible. If it stays plumb on its middle, that shows that it is fresh.

When an egg is fresh, we do not say that the only way to eat it is soft-boiled; but merely that this is the best way. Cooked thus, it loses none of its delicacy. The yolk is flavourful, the white milky; and if one has been sufficiently sybaritic to cook it in broth, and to see that it is neither over- nor under-cooked, one will eat a perfect egg.

There are people for whom an egg is an egg. This is a mistake. Two eggs which are laid at the same time, one by a hen which runs about in a garden, the other by a hen which eats straw in a farm-yard, can be very different in taste and palatability.

I am one of those who wants his egg cooked by

putting it in cold water which is then gently heated. In this way, all the egg is cooked to the same degree. If, on the contrary, you drop your egg into boiling water, it is rare that it does not break; and it can happen that the white is hard and the yolk uncooked.

If you are served with overdone eggs, as often happens, use this method: mash your eggs on a plate with salt and pepper and a piece of butter, sprinkle over them some of those chives which are called *appétits* and, if you don't have time to have other eggs cooked, you will have lost nothing on the deal.

Œufs pochés • Poached eggs

Here is the recipe from the *Cuisinier Imperial* of 1808 and the *Cuisinier Royal* of 1839. It's up to you whether to use it.

Have fifteen poached eggs, taken out of the cooking water and waiting on a platter. Have twelve ducks on the spit and, when they are 'green', that is to say nearly cooked, take them off the spit. Slit them down to the bone, take the juices, season these with salt and coarsely ground pepper, and, without allowing them to boil, pour them over your fifteen poached eggs.

Twelve ducks for fifteen eggs! What do you say to that?

Œufs au gratin

Mix together some breadcrumbs, butter, a chopped anchovy, parsley, spring onions, shallots, three egg-yolks, salt, coarse pepper and nutmeg. Sprinkle a layer of nutmeg on the bottom of an ovenproof dish, add the above mixture and let it cook gently. Break on to this gratin the quantity of eggs which you wish to serve, and cook gently. Move a hot iron ladle (*pelle rouge*) gently over the dish to make the whites set. When they are cooked, sprinkle them with salt, pepper and nutmeg.

Œufs à la tripe • Hard-boiled eggs with fried onions
Gently fry in butter some sliced onions, without allowing them to brown. Mix in half a spoonful of flour with the onions; and add a big glassful of cream, salt, pepper and nutmeg. When this mixture has slightly reduced, add the sliced hard-boiled eggs and heat through without allowing to boil.

Œufs aux champignons • Eggs with mushrooms
Poach eight fresh eggs in water. Take some mushrooms (the quantity which you would need for making a stew) and peel, wash and dice them. Cook them in water with a bouquet garni, a piece of butter into which you have worked some flour, and a little salt. When the mushrooms are cooked and the sauce reduced, bind it with four egg-yolks and cream. Add some lemon juice and serve the sauce around the eggs.

One can make the same dish with St George's agaric or with morels.

FENNEL   *FENOUIL*

A very aromatic plant of the umbelliferous family, whose seeds smell of aniseed, especially in southern Italy. Fennel is eaten like celery. It is not unusual to see working people with a bunch of fennel under the arm and making their lunch or dinner of this, accompanied by bread.

The smell, which to begin with is pleasant, becomes unpleasant because of the excessive use made of it by the Neapolitans who put it in everything.

FIGS   *FIGUES*

Despite the reputation of figs from Argenteuil, the only good figs to be had in France come from the south. The only figs which are better than those from Marseilles are those from Capodimonte, and Sicily, than which there are none better.

Figs are eaten both fresh and dried.

People who have travelled in Italy know that the biggest insult you can make to someone from Milan is to display the thumb pressed between two fingers. This is known as *faire la figue* (to flout); and this aversion to the fig derives from an occurrence which Rabelais relates as follows:

'The people of Milan, having revolted against the Emperor Frederick, expelled the Empress, his wife, from the city, forcing her to mount an old mule, facing backwards.

'When Frederick reconquered Milan, and took the rebels prisoner, he had the idea of making the executioner place a fig under the tail of this very same mule. Each of the vanquished was made to remove it from there, and present it to the executioner while saying, "*Ecco il fico!*", and then to replace it; all this under the threat of being hanged.

'Several people preferred to be hanged rather than to submit to such a humiliation, but fear of death decided most of them to do so. This is what causes the fury of the Milanese when someone "makes a fig" at them.'

It was also a fig which caused the Roman senate to decide to destroy Carthage. Every time that Cato gave his views to the senate he finished with the words, 'Carthage must be destroyed!' (*Delenda est Carthago!*).

During one session of the senate, when they were deliberating on war with Carthage, Cato showed his colleagues a fig. 'When do you think,' said he, 'this fig was picked? To judge by its freshness, very recently. Well then, only three days ago this fig was hanging from the tree, and it comes from Carthage. Judge from this how close the enemy is to us!' It was immediately decided to go to war.

Thouin, the nurseryman at the botanical gardens, ordered a very simple-minded servant to take two beautiful early figs to Buffon. On the way, the servant allowed himself to be tempted and ate one of them. Buffon, knowing that he was to have been sent two, asked the man for the other one. The latter admitted that he no longer had it.

'Well, what did you do with it?' exclaimed Buffon.

The servant took the remaining fig and, swallowing it, said: 'This is what I did with it! . . .'

FROG   *GRENOUILLE*

There are many types of frog which differ in size, colour and habitat. Frogs which live in the sea are monstrous, and are not used as a foodstuff, nor are frogs which live on the land. The only frogs which are good to eat are those which live in the water. They must be taken from very clear water, and those chosen should be well nourished, fat and fleshy, and should have a green body marked with little black spots. Many doctors in the Middle Ages were opposed to the idea of people eating this meat, which nevertheless is white and delicate and contains gelatinous matter which is more liquid and less nourishing than that of other meats. Bernard Palissy, in his *Traité des pierres* (Treatise on Stones) of 1580, expressed himself thus:

'And in my time, I have observed that there are very few men who have wanted to eat either tortoises or frogs.'

And yet in the sixteenth century frogs were served at the best tables, and Champier complained of the taste for these, which he found odd. And it is just about a century ago that a man named Simon, from Auvergne, made a considerable fortune on frogs which were sent to him from his part of the country, which he fattened and then sold to the best houses in Paris, where this food was very much in style.

In Italy and Germany, there is a very large consumption of these batracians, and the markets are covered with them. The English are horrified by them, and no doubt for this reason they used to make, about sixty years ago, caricatures showing the French eating frogs. They should read this passage from the history of the island of Santo Domingo, written by an Englishman named Atwood:

'There are', said he, 'in Martinique many toads which are eaten. The English and the French prefer them to chickens. They are fricasseed and used in soup.'

Frogs are prepared in several different ways, mostly in soups which are very health-giving and which are even used by some women to maintain the freshness of the complexion.

GINGERBREAD   *PAIN D'ÉPICE*

Since olden days the best gingerbread has been made in Reims. At the end of the fifteenth century, in the reign of Louis XII, it enjoyed a great reputation, and that made in Paris was second in rank.

Towards the end of the reign of Louis XIV and at the beginning of the reign of Louis XV it was customary to make presents of crisp biscuits and gingerbread nuts from Reims. Only children eat them now, but even so the business remains considerable.

Gingerbread is made with the best rye flour, sugar foam or yellow honey and spices. You cook it all together and then divide it up into such shapes as you wish. It stimulates the appetite and restores and sustains the digestive processes; but one must only eat it in moderation. Sailors do well to make use of it.

The invention of gingerbread goes back a long way; there is no doubt but that it followed on the heels of that of bread. Encouraged by the success of the process which produced bread, people tried combining the flours of different cereals with anything which could enhance their flavours, such as butter, eggs, milk, honey, in order to discover what the results would be. It was no doubt these experiments which gave birth to all the pastries with which the ancients regaled themselves. Our forefathers brought back the recipes for them from Egypt and Asia at the time of the Crusades; and these recipes have served to shape the art of the pastry-maker and the confectioner.

The Romans had their gingerbread; it was the offering made by the poor to the immortal gods. The Greeks ate it at the dessert course. Our own ancestors appreciated it greatly and even made use of it as gifts. It took a prominent place in meals at court. Agnès Sorel, the beautiful mistress of Charles VII, called the Lady of Beauty (because of the Château de Beauté which she owned on the banks of the Marne, and which was a present from her royal lover), never tired of this delicacy. Several authors in the last century have even suggested that the Dauphin poisoned her with gingerbread; since Louis XI liked her not at all, because his father liked her all too well. But this conjecture is based solely on the cruel and vindictive character of this prince.

Marguerite de Valois, the sister of François I, also revelled in it. But under Henri II people suddenly took a dislike to it, because rumour had it that the Italians were putting poison in it. It only came back into favour at the end of the reign of Louis XIV, as we said above.

Rye flour makes this bread a bit heavy, but when it is well prepared and properly cooked the aromatics which are used make it more digestible. Good gingerbread, preferably made with good honey and lightly spiced, has laxative qualities, quenches thirst and promotes expectoration.

In order to prevent it from becoming soggy, as a result of humidity, and from becoming stale, it must be cooked correctly and exposed from time to time to the heat of a fire or the sun.

GOOSE   *OIE*

Geese were sacred for a long time in Rome. This was because, while the dogs slept, a goose who had remained awake (history does not tell us why) heard the noise made by the Gauls in scaling the Capitol. This goose woke her friends, who all took fright and started screeching so loudly and to such good purpose that they in their turn awoke Manlius.

But as soon as Julius Caesar had defeated the Gauls, members of the Roman army started to eat geese (following in this the example of the Gauls, who had no reason to respect Manlius' allies, the cause of their downfall).

Word soon spread, even as far as Rome, that the geese from Picardy made a delicious dish. From that time on, men of Picardy, who are born traders, could be seen conducting flocks of geese to Rome on foot. Along the way, the geese devoured everything in sight.

The ancient Egyptians regarded the goose as one of the most delicate of dishes. Rhadamanthus, King of Lycia, thought so highly of them that he ordered people to stop swearing by the gods, and to swear by the goose instead, in all his lands. This was also the usual oath in England at the time when Julius Caesar conquered it.

According to Pliny, it was a Roman consul, named

Metellus Scipio, who discovered the art of fattening geese and making their livers delectable.

Jules César Scaliger, doctor and celebrated scholar, has a particularly soft spot for geese. He admires them not only from the physical, but also from the moral point of view.

'The goose,' says he, 'is the most beautiful emblem of prudence. Geese lower their heads in order to pass under a bridge, no matter how high its arches are; they are decent and reasonable to such a point that, when they are ill, they purge themselves without a doctor.

'They have so much foresight that when they pass over Mount Taurus, which abounds in eagles, each goose will take a stone in its beak. Knowing what chatterboxes they are, they ensure, by thus constraining themselves, that they will not emit the sounds which would cause their enemies to discover them.'

Geese can even be taught a little. Mémery, the chemist, saw a goose turning a spit on which a turkey was roasting. She was holding the end of the spit in her beak; and by sticking out and pulling back her neck, produced the same effect as the use of an arm. All she needed was to be given a drink from time to time.

GRAPE   *RAISIN*

Since the time of Noah, who was the first to plant and make use of the vine, innumerable varieties of grape have been produced. It would take too long to enumerate them all here, so we will limit ourselves to mentioning the principal ones, which is to say those customarily seen on our tables.

These are the *chasselas* [a fine white table grape] of Fontainebleau, which stands in the top rank. The large Corinthian and the black *chasselas* come afterwards, and a few muscats such as the one from Frontignan, the early muscat from Piédmont, that from Rivesaltes, the coral red, the big black muscat, the purple from Gascogne and the *passe-musqué* of Italy. There is also the big grape, elongated and purple, of the Madeira type, famed for its beauty, size and excellence. But the best of all the muscat grapes is that which has been given the name of *l'Enfant-Jésus* (Infant Jesus), after the beautiful painting by Mignard; unfortunately this excellent fruit has become very rare.

According to Gallienus, the grape is the best of all autumn fruits, the most nourishing of those which do not keep, and the one whose juice is the least harmful when it is completely ripe. Tissot has reported that some soldiers, attacked by an obstinate dysentery, recovered rapidly when they were conveyed to a vineyard, where they ate grapes in abundance.

Richard Lion-heart, when he was still only the Duke of Guienne, called together the notables of his Duchy, and proclaimed this memorable edict: 'Whosoever takes a bunch of grapes from another's vineyard will pay five sous or will lose an ear.' This edict teaches us that in 1175, at the time when it was given, an ear was very little valued in Gascony, since it was worth only five sous. Since then they have appreciated in value very considerably, because today there is not a single Gascon, no matter how young, who does not value his ears a great deal more than all the vineyards in the world, even though he is still very fond of the grape.

People have noticed that certain small game, such as little foxes, the hare and some small birds, become much plumper in autumn. At that time their flesh becomes more tender, delicate and better to eat, but as soon as the grape harvest is completed they become completely thin, and their flesh loses the good taste which it acquired through the grape.

The drying of grapes, in removing most of the liquid element from them and in lessening the acid which they contain, makes them more nourishing, and at the same time gives them an emollient quality very suitable for curing any acridity of the stomach, and for soothing the abdomen. So anyone suffering from a weak stomach will do well to chew two or three raisins, including the seeds, after the meal. This contributes greatly to the digestion of the food.

Grapes are dried either in the sun or in ovens. The first method keeps them very sweet, whereas the second method gives them a certain tartness. The famous Damascus raisins come from vines with large grapes, or long, oblong grapes, and are named according to the name of the place where they are grown: French raisins, Calabrian, Spanish or Levantine. Amongst Spanish raisins a distinction is made between those from the muscat grapes, sun-dried grapes (dried on the vine, in the sun), the blossoming grape, Malaga grapes and grapes from Lexias. The best raisins in France come from Languedoc and Provence; these are called *jubis, pcards* etc. So far as the raisins of Italy are concerned, those from Calabria are much acclaimed because of their excellent flesh and delicate flavour.

The very small raisins which are called *raisins de Corinthe* (currants) come from a variety of vine which grows mostly in the Ionian islands and in Greece. The alcoholic liqueur which is made by fermenting raisins and wines together was already known in the ancient world, under the name *vinum passum*, and was one of the favourite drinks of the Romans.

HAZELNUTS (also called FILBERTS)
AVELINES

A kind of large purplish nut. They say that the best kind comes from the lands of Foix and Roussillon, but I am inclined to think that the best are those from Avellines, which has given them their name. Hazelnuts grow wild in the ravines and ruins which surround Avellines. Victor Hugo all but killed himself when he fell into one of these ravines while he was picking hazelnuts as a child.

HERBS
HERBES

The twenty-eight herbs which are used in the kitchen are divided into pot-herbs (*herbes potagères*), herbs for seasoning, and herbs to accompany salads.

Pot-herbs are six in number. One should know that these are: sorrel, lettuce, white beet, orach, spinach and green purslane.

The herbs for seasoning are ten in number: parsley, tarragon, chives, spring onion, savory, fennel, thyme, basil and tansy.

Herbs to be mixed in with salad, or *fines herbes*, are twelve in number: garden cress, water cress, chervil, tarragon, burnet, samphire, buck's horn plantain, bush basil, purslane, *cordioles* of fennel, thyme, young balm and chives.

HERRING · HARENG

Everyone knows the herring. I would even say that there are few people who do not like it.

In life, the herring is green on the back, with white flanks and belly; after death the green of the back changes to blue. It is the offspring of the pole. From its birthplace to the 45th degree of latitude, it is found in all the seas. From 25 June onwards, when one begins to see in Holland [i.e. in Dutch waters] what is called 'herring lightning', the herring form long shoals which are several leagues wide and so thick that the fish which constitute them stifle each other by the thousand in shallow waters. Sometimes the nets which they fill, too weak to lift such a weight, tear apart and release their half-captured prey. By means reminiscent of the columns of fire and smoke of the Hebrews, one can keep track of the movements of the herring by day and by night; at night by the phosphorescent glow which they diffuse, during the day by the groups of fish-eating birds which follow them, swooping down from time to time and ascending again with a flash of silver in their beaks. Whales, sharks, porpoises, bonitos and sea bream pursue them, biting at the shoal itself, and consume enormous numbers of them.

The herring fishery is the most important of all, now that the fishery for cod is diminishing. This is demonstrated by Le Havre, which used to send forty vessels to fish for cod and only sent one this year. The herring industry provides a livelihood for 800,000 people and earns for Europe about 4,000,000 francs [annually].

Of the fresh herrings eaten in Paris, the most handsome and those of the best quality are the ones which come to us from the coasts of Normandy. We shall explain further on how they are prepared for table.

The freshly salted herring known as *hareng pec* should always come from Rotterdam, Leeuwarden or Enkhuizen, in Holland. This kind of herring is cut into rounds and eaten quite raw, without undergoing any kind of preparation beyond that given to a salad.

The finest *harengs saurs* (red herrings), the biggest, the most succulent, those of the most beautiful gold colour, the ones which have received the best smoking over juniper wood are the *saurets* of Germuth in Ireland [presumably a mistake for Yarmouth in England, which has for centuries been famed for its red herrings and bloaters].

Salt herrings hardly ever appear on the table of the masters; but in countries where they are plentiful they are very useful for workmen and poor people. In certain provinces people make of them an extremely appetizing and fortifying dish, thus: they do not de-salt them, but fry them in small pieces, in lard, with a mass of raw, chopped leeks, mixed with potatoes of the large floury kind, which have been cooked in well-salted water with sprigs of rosemary.

A fresh herring is an excellent fish, about which one would make the greatest fuss if it was expensive and rare. It is necessary to choose fresh herrings which have their gills red and their scales shining, and which are well rounded on the underside, for then they are full of meat; but it is only at the end of August or in mid-September that they have the fullest flavour.

In the sixteenth century there still existed, among the canons of the cathedral of Reims, quite a peculiar custom. On Ash Wednesday, after evening prayers, they used to process to the church of Saint-Rémi in two files, each trailing behind him a herring attached to a cord. Each canon tried to step on the herring of the canon in front of him, and to save his own herring from being trodden on unexpectedly by the canon behind. It was inevitable that this extravagant practice should be suppressed, along with the procession.

The herring fishery, as is well known, is one of the most productive branches of trade for England, which exports a lot of herring, especially to Italy for Holy Week. At the time when Pope Pius VII had to leave Rome, which had been conquered by the revolutionary French, the committee of the Chamber of Commerce in London was considering the herring fishery. One member of the committee observed that, since the Pope had been forced to leave Rome, Italy was probably going to become a Protestant country. 'Heaven preserve us from that!' cried another member. 'What,' responded the first, 'would you be put out to see the number of good Protestants increased?' 'No,' replied the other, 'it isn't that, but if there are no more Catholics, what shall we do with our herrings?'

Harengs frais au fenouil • Fresh herrings with fennel
Split your herrings open along the back and anoint them
with warm butter and salt, using a feather or a small
brush. Wrap them up in fennel leaves, grill them and
serve them with a *sauce rousse* to which you add some
thin stalks and leaves of fennel, previously blanched in
white wine and chopped very finely.

Harengs frais en matelote
Put your herrings in a casserole with a piece of butter,
parsley, mushrooms, spring onions, a touch of garlic,
two good glassfuls of Burgundy or Bordeaux wine, salt
and pepper. Cook them over a high heat, serve them
with the sauce reduced and with a garnish of fried croûtons.

INDIAN PICKLES   *ACHARDS*

A well-known mixture which comes to us from the East
Indies, bearing the name of its inventor. The best pickles
come from Reunion Island. All that has to be done is to
chop finely slices of pumpkin and white beet. Add to
this white onions, mushrooms, palm cabbage, cauliflower, corn which has only grown a third of the way to
maturity, etc. Colour it all with saffron, and pickle it with
salt and vinegar from Orléans, salting and peppering the
mixture as for gherkins. You complete the operation by
adding ginger root and a few red peppers.

Indian pickles are eaten in three ways. They may be
taken straight out of their jar. Or they can be cut into

pieces and mixed with all sorts of roast or boiled meats. They are also eaten after being drained on a napkin, and then impregnated with good green oil.

Finally, they are eaten dressed with cream cheese made with goat's milk, instead of with green oil. This is what is called in the colonies *à la cucoco*. This last recipe has been given to European gastronomes by le Marquis de Sercey, Vice-Admiral, and former Governor of the French Indies, to whom we are indebted for the ayapana which he first brought to France.

Achiar • Bamboo pickle
A sort of jam made with vinegar and bamboo shoots which are still green. The Dutch use this a great deal for seasoning their dishes from the East Indies, where it is made in earthenware urns. This condiment is very bitter and hot; it agrees only with people of phlegmatic temperaments and with the elderly.

JULIENNE   *JULIENNE*

This is the name given to a soup made from various sorts of herbs and vegetables, particularly carrots cut up fine. People have managed to preserve these chopped vegetables by means of drying them, thus enabling this soup to be made at any time.

From the recipes of Marc Heliot, we learn that formerly the julienne was not made exclusively of vegetables. In fact, it had among its ingredients a shoulder of mutton, which was half roasted and then put in a pot with a slice of beef, a fillet of veal, a capon and four *pigeons fuyards* [a small, pale variety of domesticated pigeon]. All this was cooked for five or six hours to make a rich bouillon. We also learn that three carrots, six turnips, two parsnips, three onions, two parsley roots, two heads of celery, three bunches of green asparagus, four handfuls of sorrel, four white lettuces and a good pinch of chervil were to be cut in pieces, with the addition, if the season permitted, of a *litron* (nearly a litre) of small green peas; all to be cooked separately from the meat in a large *marmite* containing the bouillon in which would be simmering the bread crusts which are also ingredients in this soup of olden times.

KANGAROO   *KANGUROO*

Kangaroos come originally from Australia and the surrounding islands. Essentially fruit-eaters in their wild state, kangaroos are very easy to feed when tame. They decide to eat everything which is offered to them and, it is said, even drink wine and brandy when these are given to them.

Among the mammals, the kangaroo is without question one of the animals which would be the most useful and easiest to breed in Europe, either in captivity or wild. In fact, the taming of the kangaroo, as several experiments have already shown, requires practically no trouble. This is particularly true of the large kinds of kangaroo which inhabit the southern regions of Australia and Van Diemen's Land. The climate of these provinces, although temperate in general, is often very cold, and the abundant warm hair which covers the kangaroo would allow it to withstand the most rigorous winters in France without suffering too much.

The flesh of the kangaroo is excellent, especially when it has grown up wild. The rapid growth of these animals, coupled with their considerable height, produces a substantial amount of meat in very little time. In addition, the peculiar structure of these animals, which gives them back legs much larger in size than their front ones, is eminently favourable to the production of good quality meat, greatly preferable to that of the cow or sheep in that it is much more tender than the first and much more abundant and nutritious than the second.

The kangaroo is timid and gentle. It is not in the least destructive, as several authors have claimed. In this respect it can be compared to the hare. It is very easy to feed.

The lifespan of the kangaroo is from ten to twelve years. In the final period of its existence, it very often becomes blind, because of cataracts which develop. At this stage these unfortunate creatures, no longer able to see their way, sometimes crash into the walls of their enclosures and shatter themselves to pieces.

KIDNEY   *ROGNON*

It is under the name *rognons* that the culinary art has seized on the kidneys of animals. They are characterized by a flavour of urine, which is what the connoisseurs of this sort of dish are seeking.

The meat of the kidney is distinguished by the fact

that cooking never makes it more tender. It usually has a soft and compact consistency which makes it difficult to digest and which produces obstructions. There are some young animals, however, whose kidneys are fairly tender and which have a good flavour, such as lambs, calves, suckling pigs and a few others.

Since beef kidneys are always slightly gritty and have too strong a flavour, we recommend our readers not to use them too much.

Rognons de mouton aux mousquetaires •

Mutton kidneys, musketeers' style
Take some kidneys, remove the fat, split them in two and put them on skewers. Season them with salt, pepper and a little finely chopped shallot. Grease a casserole with some butter, bacon fat or other fat, arrange the kidneys in it, and put it on the fire or hot embers for a moment, with heat above and below. Leave them for just a moment, for this is enough to cook them. Arrange them on a platter. Into the casserole in which they were cooked put a little water, a few fresh bread crumbs, salt, pepper and a dash of vinegar. Put the kidneys on to this and serve as an hors-d'oeuvre.

Rognons de veau sautés • Sautéed veal kidneys

Remove the skin and fat from the veal kidneys and chop them up. Put them in a frying pan with butter, salt, pepper, nutmeg, chopped shallot and parsley, and cooked mushrooms. Sauté all this on a very high heat. Add a little flour, some white wine and a few spoonfuls of reduced espagnole sauce. Then, just at the moment of serving, put a little very fresh butter and lemon juice on the kidneys.

If you cook veal kidneys on a spit, or in the oven, you leave the fat on.

LEPORIDE (BELGIAN RABBIT)   *LÉPORIDE*

For something like six thousand years, people have reproached scientists for fighting against God, without themselves succeeding in creating even the smallest animal.

Tired of these reproaches, they set to work, and in the year of grace 1866, they answered back by inventing the *léporide*.

This time, they not only played a trick on God, but also on M. de Buffon.

M. de Buffon had said, seeing the antipathy which exists between hares and rabbits, despite the resemblance between the two species: 'These types will never approach each other.'

M. de Buffon was wrong.

The antipathy which exists between the hare and the rabbit is not a racial antipathy, but a simple antipathy of character. If it is true that nothing resembles a hare physically more than a rabbit, it is also true that in point of character nothing resembles it less. The hare is a dreamer, or rather a day-dreamer, who has chosen the surface of the earth for his abode. He only leaves his form after taking the greatest precautions, after having turned his ears, which are like mobile funnels, in all directions. It is especially during the day that he goes on expeditions,

43

and he will not return to his form if he has been chased from it two or three times.

The rabbit, on the other hand, digs a long underground gallery, of which he alone knows all the twists and turns, and uses this as his resting place. He leaves it in imprudent fashion, not bothering about the noise which he makes in going out; and it is almost always at dusk that he risks his incautious sorties. Then, being very partial to green wheat, clover and fragrant wild thyme, he goes to look for these elegant hors d'oeuvres in the plain, as they are not to be found in the forest. It is there that the hunter lies in wait for him, and makes him pay for his lack of caution.

It has been said that the antipathy which exists between rabbits and hares is such that a warren which is invaded by rabbits is immediately abandoned by hares, and vice versa. This is perfectly true; the reason being that the rabbit, wayward and rowdy, sleeps all day and stays up all night, whereas the hare sleeps during the night and is awake by day. It is obvious that such a difference in habits makes it impossible for creatures with such dissimilar ways of life to share the same dwelling.

This, on the other hand, was just the point on which the scientists were counting. They put a litter of rabbits and hares together, before either of them had opened their eyes, and they fed them on milk from a cow, an animal which, having no connection with them, could not inculcate in them by means of their first nourishment any preconceived hatreds.

They put the two litters in a dark room so that, when the infant creatures opened their eyes, they could not distinguish the slight differences which exist between the two species.

The animals thought they all belonged to the same family and, being well fed and having no reason to quarrel, lived together in fraternal friendship until the first stirrings of love were felt by them, and were substituted for brotherly tenderness.

The scientists took turns watching, so that nothing would be missed of the coupling thought by M. de Buffon to be impossible. One day they saw, with great pleasure, a doe rabbit and a buck hare approaching each other with more than fraternal tenderness, after which the little colony promised to increase soon in such proportions as would leave no doubt at all but that the two families, which supposedly would never approach each other, were cross-breeding.

About twenty little ones were the result of this mysterious scientific experiment. However, nature prevailed, in that the female rabbits gave birth to eight or ten little ones, whereas the female hares only produced two leverets to see the light of day.

It was only a matter of continuing the experiment to give the lie completely to M. de Buffon.

M. de Buffon had said: 'If, as a result of a mistake, weakness or violence there were to be a coupling between the two species, the result would be cross-breeds who would be impotent to reproduce themselves.'

This abnormal litter was isolated from all other members of their species and, to the great satisfaction of these learned persons, the children followed the example of their fathers and continued cross-breeding.

It was left to give a name to this new species; it was called *léporide*; and steps were taken to see that the cross-breeding continued. So today we have some completely new animals, much to the delight of the learned men who created them and gave them this name.

They share at the same time the qualities of the hare and the rabbit, but they are bigger than their progenitors and weigh thirteen or fourteen pounds. Their flesh is lighter than that of the hare, but less light than that of the rabbit; they can be accompanied as you please by any of the sauces which are usually served with the two quadrupeds who took part in their creation. It seems certain that in two or three years they will become common enough to take an honourable place in our forests and in our markets. I have even been assured that some have already been seen in the market places of Le Mans and Anjou. One was sent to me by the *Société d'Acclimatation* [see page 62] on the express understanding that I would eat it. I can confirm that whether it was the son of a buck rabbit and a doe hare or of a doe rabbit and a buck hare, it was in no way inferior to either its mother or its father.

[No more has been heard of the leporide. Expert opinion suggests that M. de Buffon was right and that the animal never existed; or that, if it did, it was unable to reproduce. Work in this field in the present century is thus summed up by Annie P. Gray (*Mammalian Hybrids*, Commonwealth Agricultural Bureaux, Slough, 2nd edition, 1972): 'There are conflicting opinions on the possibility of this cross, but controlled experiments have invariably given negative results.']

LOBSTER   *HOMARD*

The lobster is a crustacean much used in cooking. The *langouste*, or spiny lobster, is less flavourful and less prized; its meat can be chopped and put in a mayonnaise, to produce an excellent white sauce for bass and turbot.

In Paris one must, so far as possible, buy only live lobsters. Choose, moreover, the heaviest that you can find; and put it to cook in a copper pan or casserole with salted water, a big piece of fresh butter, a bunch of parsley sprigs, a red pimento and two or three white leeks. After a quarter of an hour's cooking, add a goblet of Madeira or Marsala, and leave the lobster to cool in the court-bouillon. The segments of shell must then be cut along the whole length of the tail; and you will already have made a sauce, for which the following is the best recipe.

Take out in a single piece the whole of the interior of the lobster known as the *tourteau* and detach all the white meat with a sharpened quill. Take out the 'stuffing' or creamy roe which is to be found attached to the carapace. Add the eggs of the lobster, if it is female, and mix all this together with green olive oil, a generous spoonful of good mustard, ten or twelve drops of Chinese soya sauce, a handful of chopped fines herbes, two crushed shallots, a fair amount of black pepper, and finally a liqueur glass of *anisette* from Bordeaux or simply of aniseed ratafia. Beat it all together with a fork as you would an omelette, and, depending on the size of the lobster, add the juice of two or three lemons to the sauce.

Homard à la broche • Lobster on a spit

Take a large lobster or spiny lobster, alive and vigorous, and fix it on a stout skewer, which you then tie with string on to a spit. Expose it right away to a hot fire, having sprinkled it with champagne and melted butter, salt and pepper. The shell will quickly become crisp, that is to say apt to crumble between the fingers, like chalk. When it becomes detached from the body, this is the sign that the lobster is sufficiently cooked; it must then be sprinkled again with the juice from the dripping pan, from which the fat has been skimmed and to which has been added the juice of a Seville orange and a pinch of mixed spices.

This ragoût, which is peculiar to Normandy, never fails to create an impression when it appears on the table.

[Dumas gives, under the same heading of Lobster, an account of a whole meal which he prepared at the seaside.]

'Oh sea, the only love to whom I have been faithful'

This line from Byron may become my motto, and I love the sea and hold it as necessary to our pleasure and even to the happiness of our existence. When a certain period of time has elapsed since I have seen the sea, I am tormented by an irresistible desire and, under some pretext or other, I take the train and arrive either at Trouville, Dieppe or Le Havre. On one particular day, I had gone to Fécamp.

I had hardly arrived before a fishing expedition was proposed for the following day.

I know all about fishing expeditions where nothing is caught, but one buys the fish which forms the basis of the dinner after the fishing expedition. On this occasion, however, contrary to the usual practice, we caught two mackerel and an octopus, but we bought a lobster, a plaice and about a hundred shrimps. A woman selling mussels, whom we encountered on our way, added to this lot about a hundred of her bivalves.

We had been having long discussions to establish to whose house we would repair and who consequently would be in charge of the dinner. Finally the choice fell on a wine merchant from Fécamp who had put his entire cellar at our disposition. He assured us en route that his cook had got the *pot-au-feu* going, and that we would find at his house the wherewithal for two or three dishes which the cook would have gotten together for his own dinner.

But his cook, even though he claimed her to be a cordon bleu, was unanimously demoted and I was elected in her place. She was free to keep the title of vice-cook, but only on condition that she would not oppose the chief cook in any way.

As we had been promised, we found a *pot-au-feu* which had been simmering since ten o'clock that morning, which meant that it had had about eight hours of cooking time. And it is after eight hours of cooking that a *pot-au-feu* comes of age.

France, I have already said, is the only country which knows how to make a *pot-au-feu*; furthermore, it is probable that my janitress, who has nothing to do but look after her *pot-au-feu* and unlatch the door, eats better soup than M. Rothschild.

To come back to our cook, she had the *pot-au-feu* which was simmering, two chickens already plucked and awaiting the spit, a beef kidney still ignorant of the sauce for which it was destined, a bunch of asparagus which was starting to run to seed, and at the bottom of her basket some tomatoes and white onions.

I had everything spread out on the kitchen table, and I asked for pen and ink. For the approval of my table companions I presented the following menu:

Potage aux tomates et aux queues de crevettes.

Entrées.

Homard à l'américaine.

Carrelet sauce normande.

Maquereaux à la maître d'hôtel.

Rognons sautés au vin de Champagne.

Rôts.

Deux poulets à la ficelle.

Poulpe frit.

Entremets.

Tomates à la provençale.

Oeufs brouillés au jus de rognon.

Pointes d'asperges.

Coeurs de laitue à l'espagnole, sans huile ni vinaigre.

Dessert de fruits.

Vins.

Château-d'Iquem, Corton, Pommard, Château-Latour.

Café.

Bénédictine. Fine champagne.

As I said, I presented the menu, which was greeted with enthusiastic cheers. The only question which arose was how long it would take me to prepare such a dinner.

I asked for an hour and a half, which was granted me with some astonishment. They had thought it would take three.

The great talent of a cook who wants to be ready on time is to prepare as much as possible in advance and to have all the necessary ingredients readily to hand. This takes but a quarter of an hour. Now, as it is impossible in writing about the meal to set going a soup, four entrées, two roasts, two side dishes and a salad, all at the same time, allow me to take up and explain my courses dish by dish.

Potage aux tomates et aux queues de crevettes ·
Tomato and shrimp bisque
In one pan, heat salted water for the shrimps, with assorted herbs and two slices of lemon. When it is boiling, throw in the shrimps.

In a second pan, put twelve tomatoes from which you have pressed out the excess liquid, four big onions cut in rounds, a piece of butter, a clove of garlic and assorted herbs. [Cook all this together.]

When the shrimps are cooked, drain them in a colander, keeping the cooking water. Peel the shrimps and put the peeled tails aside.

Once the tomatoes and onions are cooked, press them through a fine sieve, put them back on the fire with a little jellied meat stock and a pinch of red pepper, and let this thicken into a purée. Then add an equal quantity of bouillon, and half a glass of the water in which the shrimps were cooked, and bring to the boil while stirring. When it has boiled up three or four times, toss in the shrimps, and the soup is ready.

By the way, although I am giving each recipe separately, it will be obvious that everything has to be cooking at the same time.

Homard à l'américaine • Lobster *à l'américaine*
We are choosing Vuillemot's method from the various different methods for preparing lobster *à l'américaine*.

We beseech our readers, and above all the ladies, to pay great attention, as the dish is very complicated.

1. Prepare in a casserole two large onions cut in quarters, a bouquet of assorted herbs and two scraps of garlic; add a bottle of good white wine, half a glass of ordinary cognac, a ladleful of good consommé, salt, ground pepper and several grains of good cayenne pepper from Spain. Then toss in your lobster. Half an hour of cooking will suffice.

But wait a minute! The most difficult part is still to be done.

2. Let your crustacean cool in the cooking water, if you are not in a hurry; and the less hurried you are, the better it will be. Then remove the meat from the lobster, including the meat from the claws, and cut it all up into neat slices. Put all this in a sauce-boat, moisten it with a little of the bouillon in which the lobster was cooked, cover with a piece of buttered paper and keep it in a warming oven. You must wait before serving it.

3. Take eight beautiful tomatoes and cut each in half. Press out and discard the watery part. Butter a casserole

and lay your tomatoes on this, seasoning them with salt, ground pepper, a little cayenne and fresh butter. Put the casserole in the oven and, after cooking, keep it hot.

4. Take two big onions, dice them, squeeze them in a cloth to extract the gluten, sauté them in a casserole with a little butter until they are golden, add a tablespoon of flour and then add half the bouillon in which the lobster was cooked. Let your sauce refine at the side of the stove and reduce it by half, adding two generous spoonfuls of tomato purée. Reduce again by a third, adding some jellied meat stock. Next, strain the sauce, add a bit of lemon juice, a nut of fresh butter, and wait.

5. Finally, take the lobster's coral, and the eggs if it has any, pound all this in a mortar with some butter, sieve it and add a little cayenne. Take a vegetable dish and arrange the pieces of lobster in it in the shape of a crown, with the tomatoes on top. Pour the lobster butter into the gaps between the pieces of lobster, glaze with some meat essence and serve.

As this dish is somewhat complicated, it should not be attempted by novices; one must be a real cook, equipped with a certain skill, in order to attack it.

Carrelet à la sauce normande •

Plaice with *sauce normande*

Put the plaice on a silver dish, which must be buttered, season it with salt, pepper and a glass of white wine and put it in the oven.

Put a piece of butter in a casserole and stir in a little flour, until it becomes golden. Moisten this with the butter and white wine from the plaice, leaving behind only enough liquid to ensure that it does not dry up. Reduce by half.

Cook about thirty mussels and ten or twelve mushrooms. Put the juice from the mussels in the sauce, reduce it all by half, then bind it with four egg yolks and half a glass of fresh cream. Arrange the mussels and mushrooms around the plaice and pour the sauce on top. Dot the dish here and there with some little pieces of very fresh butter, let the fish sit in the oven for two minutes, then serve it.

* * *

As to the mackerel *à la maître d'hôtel* and the sautéed kidneys with Burgundy wine, I can't teach anyone anything about making these two dishes. They are the ABC of cooking. The only thing is, take care to make the sauce for the kidneys rather thin, and put half a glass of this to one side at the time of serving. You will see why later.

Poulets à la ficelle

Up to the time when I came to make my chicken *à la ficelle*, I had put up with the comments of my vice-cook, but once we arrived at this decisive moment her comments turned into opposition.

As I had no time to waste, I threatened her with a *coup d'état*, offering to have her wages paid and then to have her sacked immediately. This threat had its effect. She obeyed passively, and five minutes later, my two chickens were turning side by side like two spindles.

But, as I have more time today, listen to me and let me explain why chicken cooked *à la ficelle* is superior to spit-roasted chicken.

All animals have two orifices, the upper and the lower. The chicken, in this respect, is the same as man. Diogenes said it two thousand four hundred years before me, on the day when he threw down in the Agora at Athens a feathered cock, shouting: 'Here is Plato's man.'

Well, first one must stop up one of the orifices, the upper one. This orifice is blocked up in the Belgian fashion, by poking the head of the bird into its stomach and sewing up the skin on top.

Let us move on to the second orifice, the lower one, which is much more important than the first.

You will have removed (and when I say you will have removed, I mean that your cook will have removed) the intestines and the liver. She will have thrown away the intestines, chopped up the liver with fines herbes, spring onions and parsley, and worked this together with a piece of butter. She will have replaced the intestines, which now are not only useless, but actually harmful, with this minced mixture which is destined to give the chicken added flavour.

Now, what should the aim of the cook be? To preserve the greatest possible quantity of juices in the animal which is to be cooked. Now, if you pass a skewer lengthways through the animal and, to keep it in place, pass another one through the animal crossways, then instead of stopping up one of the two holes which nature has made you have added two more holes, from which all the animal's juices will escape.

If, on the contrary, you tie its feet with a string, and hang it up vertically by this string, with the lower orifice up in the air and the upper orifice stopped up, and if you baste the chicken with best quality fresh butter into which you have worked salt and pepper, taking care to tip some into the lower orifice with the basting spoon, you will have fulfilled all the logical requirements for having an excellent chicken. The only thing left for you to do is to keep an eye on it while it is cooking, and then, when you see a few little cracks appear in its skin, from which issue jets of steam, cut the string. At this point put the chicken in the dripping pan, and pour the pan juices over it.

Never, never allow a single drop of bouillon to be mixed with the butter with which you baste the chicken. Any cook, as I think I have said elsewhere, any cook, I say, who puts bouillon in the dripping pan deserves to be thrown out of the door ignominiously and without mercy.

* * *

Pieuvre frite • Fried octopus

Cut your octopus into pieces, roll these in flour, slip them into boiling fat, remove when cooked, and you will have something similar to fried calves' ears, with a light taste of musk.

* * *

As for the scrambled eggs with kidney gravy and asparagus tips and tomatoes stuffed *à la provençale*, that is child's play.

Put twelve egg yolks and six egg whites into a soup tureen. After having beaten them, add a piece of butter, fines herbes, half a glass of bouillon (chicken bouillon if you have any) and the half glass of kidney juices which you have kept, and turn all this over to the cook, who has nothing more to do than to pour the mixture into a casserole, put it on the fire and stir.

Essential advice: serve the scrambled eggs soft, as they will continue to cook on the platter.

* * *

As for the tomatoes, cut them in half, let the liquid drain off, remove the seeds, put the tomatoes side by side in a *four de campagne* and pile in a pyramid, in the middle of each tomato, a mixture of chopped chicken, veal, game from the night before if you have some, and mushrooms.

Over all this pour a whole glass of olive oil, the best quality you can find; sprinkle with salt, pepper, parsley and garlic chopped up together and add a dash of pimento. Cook with heat above and below, basting the pyramids of meat three or four times with the oil in which the tomatoes are cooking.

* * *

As for the salad of hearts of lettuce, without oil or vinegar, this is a reminder of our trip to Spain. In Spain, the vinegar does not smell at all; but, in contrast, their oil is foul. As a result it is impossible, even when the heat from the sky and the dryness of the air give you the most violent longing for fresh greenery, to eat salad there.

Well, we remedied all that by substituting egg yolks for the oil, and lemon for the vinegar. This mixture, seasoned sufficiently with salt and pepper, produced an exquisite salad. We finished up by preferring its flavour to that of our French salads.

* * *

At the end of an hour and a half, the meal was on the table. The only thing was that four hours later we were still at dinner!

So, what a reputation did I leave at Fécamp, and what a reception was given to me when I arrived there for my most recent visit.

* * *

Allow me to add one more recipe which can perfectly well come after those given above, without being out of place. This is scrambled eggs with shrimps.

Take twelve eggs and break them into a salad bowl, using all the yolks, but only eight of the whites. If there is too much egg white, it detracts from the delicacy of the dish.

In a separate pan boil the bodies [minus the tails, which you reserve] of the shrimps, adding a glass of Chablis wine. Have it all bubble up two or three times, then pour everything into a mortar to make a purée of it. This you then press through a fine sieve, to remove even the smallest bits of carapace.

Blend this fine purée with the eggs to which you have already added salt and pepper and which you have lightly decorated with finely chopped spring onions and parsley. Next add to this the [peeled] shrimp tails, beat them up with the eggs and pour everything into a frying pan which has been buttered with good fresh butter. Cook, and turn out carefully on a platter.

MACKEREL   *MAQUEREAU*

One of the most handsome and one of the bravest fish in existence. When it is brought into the boat, alive, from the line, it seems to be made of azure, silver and gold.

The mackerel often attacks fish much bigger than itself, and even man. A Norwegian historian tells the story of a sailor who was bathing and suddenly disappeared. When he was fished out of the water ten minutes later he had already been largely eaten by mackerel.

These fish gather together each year to make extensive journeys. Towards the spring, they skirt the coasts of Iceland, Shetland, Scotland and Ireland and rush headlong into the Atlantic Ocean, where one column, passing in front of Portugal and Spain, goes on to enter the Mediterranean, while another column enters the English Channel, in April and May, and passes on from there, in June, to the waters off Holland and Friesland.

Mackerel are found in all the seas, in uncountable numbers. They pass the winter in the Arctic, their heads buried in the mud and fucus – that, anyway, is what people used to believe. However, Bloch, Noël, Lacépède and others think that the migrations of the mackerel are like those of the tunny and the herring, and that the former, like the latter, simply withdraw into the depths of the sea, at the surface of which they are seen to reappear in the spring.

Maquereaux à l'anglaise

Take three or four extremely fresh mackerel, gut them through the gill-openings, tie up the head of each and cut off the small tail-end; but do not cut their backs at all. Put a good handful of fennel into a poissonière which has its removable rack in place, and place the mackerel on top, adding some lightly salted water. Cook them over a low fire. Once they are cooked, lift out the rack, drain the fish, arrange them on your serving platter and pour over them a fennel sauce or the sauce called *à gro-seilles à maquereau*. [The latter sauce is gooseberry sauce. Dumas gives a recipe for it, which we have not translated, in his entry for Sauces, and describes it as an English sauce. This is interesting, since it has been known in both France and England for a long time as a suitable accompaniment for mackerel, and there are those who think that it was originally French. Dumas' method of making it, in summary form, is to take two good handfuls of half-ripe gooseberries, cut them in two, seed them, blanch them in lightly salted water and drain them. They are then added to a sauce which has been made by combining equal quantities of velouté and butter, heating the mixture and blending it well.]

MELON   *MELON*

An annual creeping plant belonging to the cucumber family. Depending on the species, the fruit is as big as either an apple or a pumpkin. Those from Honfleur sometimes weigh up to 24 pounds. They say that it grows wild in the country of the Kalmuks; but I have been there during the months of October and November without ever seeing a single melon, even though 50 leagues away they were being harvested by the thousand beside the Caspian Sea, where the biggest and the best only cost 4 sous.

The melon probably came originally from Africa. It certainly originated in hot countries and is only good when it has been caressed by the sun's rays. The best melon is the cantaloup, brought back from Armenia by the Romans; it was named thus from the village of Cantaloupo, where it was cultivated. Throughout all the southern part of France, we have the water melon or the green melon, which, for some gastronomes, equals the cantaloup.

Naples has its national melon, which is called *Cocméro*, and which is eaten almost exclusively, along with macaroni, by the *lazzaroni*. Its flesh is red, with black seeds; actually, however, it has no body, and is just cold water.

To make the melon digestible, gastronomes say that one must eat it with pepper and salt, and drink on top of it a half glass of Madeira, or rather Marsala, since Madeira has disappeared. There is no other way to prepare it but to cut it in slices and to serve it between the soup and the beef or between cheese and dessert.

NIGHTINGALE   *ROSSIGNOL*

In vain does the nightingale charm us with its melodious song. It does not stop our cruel hunters from killing it for its meat, which yields only to that of the fig-pecker in delicacy.

It is said that Lucullus had several platters of a large quantity of nightingales' brains served to him in the course of a sumptuous repast; an exquisite dish if this was so.

NOUGAT

NOUGAT

White nougat, called nougat of Marseilles, is made of sweet almond slivers and shelled pistachios which are cooked with honey from Narbonne. White nougat is served and eaten with the dessert.

Brown nougat, with which temples, domes, and porticoes are built is made as follows. Take five hundred grams of sweet almonds, shell, skin and wash them, then drain them on a white cloth. Cut each of these almonds in slivers, which you then allow to turn golden in a very slow oven. Melt 75 grams of powdered sugar in a pan on the stove. When it has completely melted, toss in your hot almonds, and mix everything together well. When you have taken the pan off the fire, put the almonds in a mould which you have wiped out and oiled. Arrange them around the mould by using a lemon to press them in place. If you use your fingers, they will stick to them. Mount them as thinly as possible, unmould them, arrange them and serve.

OMELETTE

OMELETTE

Omelette aux fines herbes

Break some eggs into a salad bowl, and beat them with a wicker beater. Add parsley, tarragon and chives to the eggs, and beat until the whites and yolks are completely blended. Pour half a glass of cream into the mixture, and beat it once more. Then, when your butter starts to bubble in the frying pan, pour the mixture in. The eggs will spread foaming to the whole circumference of the frying pan. When this happens, use a fork to keep bringing the edges back into the middle, while taking care that the omelette remains liquid, and that the cooked mixture does not become thick.

Have a platter ready which has been buttered with the freshest possible butter and sprinkled with some more fresh fines herbes. Turn out the omelette on to this platter and serve it while it is still dribbling.

Excuse the use of this last word, but each art has its own language which must be employed to make oneself understood by the initiated.

Omelette arabe • Arab omelette

I have said that my first preoccupation in writing this book was to demonstrate the cuisine of peoples who have none. Here, for example, is a recipe which the Bey's cook was kind enough to give me.

Ostrich and flamingo eggs, full and fresh, are now to be found almost everywhere, thanks to the zoological societies which have been founded even in towns of secondary importance. [The Société d'Acclimatation was founded in 1854. In 1874 the magazine which it sponsored expressed, among other aims, the intention of domesticating exotic animals and of selling to members of the society unusual products such as, one would suppose, ostrich and flamingo eggs.] Thus an ostrich egg is today sold for one franc, and is equal in content to about ten hen's eggs.

This is how to make an Arab omelette.

Chop a fresh onion, put it in a frying pan with half a glass of olive oil, let it soften without colouring, and add the flesh of two large sweet peppers, after having grilled them for a few moments in order to remove the skin.

Add two good peeled and seeded tomatoes, cut in small pieces. Season this first preparation with a little salt and a touch of cayenne. Reduce some of the liquid given off by the tomatoes, then take the frying pan off the fire and add to its contents four anchovy fillets.

Now, as a separate operation, rub the bottom of a terrine with a clove of garlic. Pierce an ostrich or flamingo egg at both ends, so that you can blow out the white and the yolk, causing them to fall into the terrine. Season, and beat with a fork.

Finally, pour a quarter of a glass of olive oil into an omelette pan. When it is thoroughly hot, pour in the eggs, let the omelette set, and add to it the mixture which you prepared earlier. Turn it over, keeping it flat; sprinkle a little more oil over it; and two seconds later slide it on to a round platter.

Omelette aux fraises • Strawberry omelette
Choose big *ananas* strawberries, which are very fresh and sweet smelling. Remove a score of the most beautiful, and cut them into quarters. Put them in a bowl with sugar, a little orange zest, and two soupspoons of rum.

Press the remaining strawberries through a fine sieve. Make enough purée to fill a glass, sweeten it sufficiently, add a little orange-flavoured sugar, and chill it on ice.

Break ten eggs into a pan. Mix into them two soupspoons of castor sugar, and two spoonfuls of good cream. Beat all this together for a few seconds with a whisk.

In a frying pan melt 150 grams of best quality butter. When it is hot, add the eggs, and let the omelette thicken with the help of a spoon. Bring it back to the front of the stove and put the strawberries which have been cut up in the middle of the omelette. Fold the omelette back at the two edges to give it a pretty shape. Sprinkle it lightly with vanilla sugar, and then place it like an island in the middle of the strawberry purée.

OYSTERS   *HUITRES*

The oyster is one of the most deprived molluscs in the kingdom of nature.

Being acephalic, that is to say having no head, it has neither an organ of sight, nor an organ of hearing, nor an organ of smell. Its blood is colourless. Its body adheres to the two valves of its shell by a powerful muscle, with the aid of which it opens and closes the shell.

It also lacks an organ of locomotion. Its only exercise is sleep and its only pleasure is to eat. Since the oyster cannot go and look for its food, its food comes to find it or is carried to it by the movement of the waters. This food consists of animal matter suspended in the water.

It has been said that 'the Gods are going away'; an eloquent exclamation and one which has been admired. But recently a cry has made itself heard that: 'The oysters are going away!' There is, to be sure, no connection between the hermaphrodite mollusc which lives in its shell at the bottom of the sea, attached for ever to its rock, and the inhabitants of the worshipful Mount Olympus. However, the famous cry of Bossuet, his famous and eloquent cry – 'Madam is dying! Madam is dead!' – did not produce an impression as terrible as this gastronomic call of distress: 'The oysters are going away!' And the first effect of this cry was to make the price of oysters go up from 60 centimes a dozen to 1 franc 30 centimes.

Feelings ran deep. The oyster, this treasure of the gourmands, was on the point of escaping from them; the oyster which, according to Dr Reveillé-Paris, is the only alimentary substance which does not cause indigestion.

We first hear of oysters among the ancient Greeks, and the very first time, I think, was in connection with the proscription of Aristides. 'I am tired of hearing him called Aristides the Just,' said an honest Athenian; and Aristides was proscribed by a majority of oysters, each oyster-shell [which was put in the ballot-box] carrying its sentence and representing the casting of a vote.

The Greeks had oysters brought from the Hellespont. They used to be gathered around Sestos, the place where Leander leaped into the sea to make his nocturnal visit to Hero. This place is known now as Boralli-Calessi. I ate some oysters from Sestos while crossing the Bosphorus, and found them nothing special.

The Romans, whose gourmandise was quite different from that of the Greeks, rendered almost divine honours to the oyster. There was no good dinner without raw oysters chilled with ice, or without cooked oysters seasoned with *garum*, a kind of brine [in fact a kind of salty fish sauce] of which Pliny has preserved the recipe for us.

The Romans graded oysters by number, according to their excellence. The first in quality were those from the Lucrine lake; then came those of Tarentum, followed by those of Circei. Later, the Romans came to prefer the oysters from the coasts of Great Britain.

Apicius, the famous gourmand who cut his throat

because he only had between six and eight million sesterces left, that is to say between fifteen hundred thousand and two million francs, had discovered a way of preserving oysters. In our time, he would have patented this and lived off the patent.

In France the oysters are fished with a dredge, and the fishermen used to make a practice of dividing the oyster banks into several zones, which were opened successively to fishing, so that the banks would not be exhausted. While one of these zones was being exploited, the other, that is to say the reserved area, would be producing more oysters which could reach marketable size.

During the months of May, June, July and August, the fishery was forbidden. Gourmands say that oysters should not be eaten in the months without an 'R'. By way of compensation, these are the months when mussels are in a state of perfection.

Oysters straight from the sea are never eaten. At least, no disciple of Lucullus or apostle of Brillat-Savarin would commit such a heresy. Oysters must be kept in special 'parks', at a depth of one metre and on sand or shingle, before being eaten.

It was a Roman called Sergius Orata, who lived 250 years before Jesus Christ, who first had the idea of putting oysters in the Lucrine lake, to fatten them. He conducted a trade in oysters, brought to a state of perfection by his careful treatment, and became a rich man.

The oyster which we eat is the *Ostrea edulis*. The Ostend oyster, the green oyster, the oyster of Marennes, all these are only varieties of the same species. [This was true, but other species, especially the Portuguese oyster, are now cultured in France and may also become, for example, *vertes de Marennes*.]

We had oyster parks at Marennes, Tréport, Étretat, Fécamp, Dunquerque, Le Havre and Dieppe. We shall come in a moment to that of Régneville. [This moment, quite a long one, is taken up by recalling the origins of pisciculture in China, its development by the Romans, and subsequent advances in the art; all portrayed as providing inspiration for M. de Chaillé and Madame Sarah-Félix, who set up an oyster park at Régneville, and whose initial problems in the enterprise are described. These lead to an account of reproduction in the oyster.]

The eggs of the oyster are almost invisible. Leuwenhoeck has worked out that about a million of them would be needed to constitute the volume of a child's marble. The tiny oysters, when they come out of their mother's shell, are capable of movement. Nature provides this faculty for the larvae of all stationary animals, and thus allows them to affix themselves where they wish. Only they must choose their abode with care; for, once fixed in it, they are stuck with it for the rest of their lives.

In the park at Régneville, they began by using ordinary tiles and bundles of sticks; thus offering the oysters a choice between a position on the sea bed and one of suspension between high and low tide. But our oyster-rearers quickly saw that they had made a twofold mistake. The bundles of twigs became coated with a mucus which made it impossible for the little oysters to attach themselves. As for the tiles, they on the contrary allowed the oysters to affix themselves too securely. The oysters found it convenient to use the tiles as one of their shells; and, when one plucked an oyster from its beloved tile, its shell was either broken or left behind on the tile. The oysters' motto was becoming that of the ivy: 'Where I attach myself, there I die.'

Our oyster-rearers then stuck old newspapers on to the tiles, so that they adhered to the tiles only by their ends. The oyster, admittedly, was now stuck to the newspaper; but the newspaper was not effectively stuck to anything. Besides, not all newspapers, in our opinion, are suitable for being used in this way. I know some which would bestow on the innocent molluscs the toxic properties which oysters at Venice contract when they attach themselves to the copper parts of boats.

What is the length of an oyster's life? This is still a mystery. To begin with, few oysters die of old age. And those who do, perish unknown.

Oysters are usually eaten in the simplest way in the world. One opens them, extracts them, sprinkles a few drops of lemon juice on them and swallows them. [Dumas does not mention the advice offered by many experts, which is to bite an oyster before swallowing it, thus releasing the flavour which is in its liver.] The most refined gourmands prepare a kind of sauce with vinegar, pepper and shallot and dip the oysters in this before swallowing them. Others – and these are the true oyster-lovers – add nothing at all to the oysters, but eat them raw without vinegar, lemon or pepper.

PARSLEY   *PERSIL*

Parsley is the obligatory condiment for all sauces.

'Parsley', says the learned author of the *Traité des plantes usuelles*, 'makes dishes more healthful and more agreeable; it stimulates the appetite and aids the digestion.' Bosc's opinion of this plant is even more positive. 'Take away parsley from the cook,' says he, 'and you render it virtually impossible for him to practise his art.'

Parsley, we repeat, is essential for all stews and all sauces; but there are two dressings in which it is the principal ingredient, that of *Watter-Fisch* and Parsley Sauce *à la Hollandaise*.

PARSNIP   *PANAIS*

This plant belongs to the same family as the carrot. Its root is white, its stem long, straight, thick, firm, ridged, hollow and branching. The flowers are of a generous size; the flavour is mild and sweet.

There are two kinds of parsnip, the long sort and the round sort. This root vegetable goes into broths; and it is also fried in butter. Its taste is not generally pleasing. Ray says that the English think that when the parsnip is too old it produces delirium and even madness; and so they call it the mad parsnip. This same plant was also said to be an aphrodisiac. It is not to be confused with hemlock, whose leaves have red spots at the base of the stems.

In Thuringia, a syrup which replaces sugar is extracted from the parsnip. It is a plant which has a composition similar to that of the beetroot and the carrot; sugar is a constituent part. Drappies says that he has extracted 12 per cent of sugar from it.

In Germany they grow and often eat a sort of farinaceous and sweet parsnip of small size. It is used to make a stew with fresh loin of pork and fillets of hind.

PASTRY   *PATISSERIE*

The character of pastry varies according to the taste and customs of the various peoples who consume it. Each people, each province, each locality has contributed successful methods to this art. They have made contributions to its enormous success by providing inventions of greater or lesser originality; but each one of these has its own distinctive character. France marches at the head of pastry making, in the present state of civilization, followed by Italy and Switzerland. Even the position of the pastry cook in our society has changed. This artist, who earlier belonged to a low class, now enjoys considerable respect. In bygone days it was proverbially said of an impudent person that he had 'passed through the *pâtissier*'s front door'. This stemmed from the fact that pastry cooks kept an inferior kind of tavern. Because it was shameful to frequent them, prudish people only entered by the back door, and it was a brazen act to go in through the shop or the front door. Today it would be an insult to equate our pretty and elegant *pâtisseries* with inferior taverns. Men of the highest breeding and women from the best social classes do not blush in entering a pastry shop, in tasting quite openly the products of the pastry-cook's labours, in savouring the excellent wines and liqueurs which he has chosen to accompany them, and in leaving his premises without shame or pretence.

PEPPER   *POIVRE*

Pepper has always been, of all known spices, the most widespread and the one most used in cooking.

For a long time pepper was an item of very great luxury, and a pound of pepper was a very considerable present to give anyone. It has been reported that, when Clotharius III founded the monastery of Corbie, thirty pounds of pepper figured among the various commodities which he required his customs authorities to pay to the monks annually.

When Roger, Count of Béziers, was assassinated in a riot by the citizens of that town in 1107, one of the punishments which his son imposed on these citizens, after he had subdued them by force of arms, was the exaction of a tribute of three pounds of pepper annually from each family. Finally, at Tyre, the Jews were obliged likewise to pay over two pounds of pepper a year to the archbishop. According to the *Annales de l'Eglise d'Aix*, it was Bertrand and Rostang de Noves, who were Archbishops of Tyre in 1143 and 1283 respectively, who imposed this obligation on the perfidious Jews.

Pepper, much used as a condiment, facilitates digestion.

Before the advent of cubeb it was frequently used in dispensaries. In hot countries, tremendously strong fermented sauces are made of it. As it is one of the most powerful stimulants, it is only used in moderation in good cooking; and nervous, susceptible people should even abstain from using it. This does not apply to country people, the sensibility of whose stomachs has become dulled by their habitually eating coarse food, and which therefore needs to be strongly excited. Pepper is just right to produce this effect; so it is much used in all provincial cooking. There are three kinds of pepper; black pepper, white pepper and long pepper.

PLUM PUDDING   *PLUM-PUDDING*

A farinaceous dish without which one cannot have a really good meal in England. It has also become much more widely served in France during these last years. For making this, the ingredients which stand first in line, as essential and constituent elements, are flour, eggs and butter, the flavour of which is enhanced by the addition of various other ingredients. Thus there is pudding with cherries, pudding with sago, lemon pudding, cauliflower pudding, frothy pudding, etc.

POTATO   *POMME DE TERRE*

This excellent vegetable was brought from Virginia by the English admiral Walter Raleigh in 1585, and since then has preserved people from famine.

This admiral was better known for his enterprising spirit and the vicissitudes of his life than he has been for the importation of the potato. This, at first, drew very little attention. Walter Scott reports that one day when Raleigh found himself taking a walk with Queen Elizabeth and her suite she had to walk a short distance through a small pool of mud. He unfastened his velvet cloak, which was embroidered with pearls, and spread it over the mud so that the queen could traverse it without wetting her feet. She rewarded him for this by naming him admiral.

As for the potato, absurd prejudices prevented it from being duly appreciated for a long time. Many people thought it a dangerous foodstuff, or at least a coarse one and at best suitable for pigs. This was the position at the end of the last century, when Parmentier began a series of practical and theoretical works which bore on the cultivation of the potato. He was sufficiently successful to overcome the prejudices, and everyone became convinced of the advantages of potato cultivation.

In 1793 potatoes were considered so indispensable that a decree of the Commune, dated 21 *Ventôse*, ordered a census to be taken of luxury gardens, so that they could be devoted to the cultivation of this vegetable. As a result, the principal avenue in the Jardin des Tuileries and the flower beds were turned over to potato cultivation. This is why potatoes were for a long time given the additional name of 'royal oranges'.

The potato is a real nourishment and one which is healthful, easy and inexpensive. Its preparation has this agreeable and advantageous aspect for the working class, that it involves practically no trouble or expense. The alacrity with which one observes children eating baked potatoes, and feeling all the better for them, proves that they suit all dispositions.

The choice of potatoes is neither in doubt, nor unimportant. The grey ones with gritty skins are the less good; the best, without question, are the purplish ones, known in Paris by the name *Vitelottes*, and preferable even to the red ones.

Pommes de terre à la parisienne

Melt a piece of butter or other fat in a casserole with one or two onions cut in small pieces. Add a glass of water, and put in your carefully peeled potatoes, with salt, pepper, and a bouquet garni, and cook on a low flame.

Pommes de terre à l'anglaise

Carefully wash some potatoes, cook them in salted water, and then peel them. Soften a good piece of butter in a casserole, put in the potatoes (which you have sliced), add salt, pepper and *mignonette* [a muslin sachet containing red pepper, nutmeg, coriander, cinnamon, ginger and cloves], but without the nutmeg. Toss the potatoes with this and serve on a very hot platter.

Pommes de terre à la provençale

Put six soupspoons of oil in a casserole with the zest of the skin of half a lemon, parsley, garlic, and well-chopped spring onion, a little grated nutmeg, salt and pepper. Then peel the potatoes, and cook them with these seasonings. When the moment to serve arrives, sprinkle them with the juice of a lemon.

QUARTER OF DEER, ENGLISH STYLE
QUARTIER DE DAIM À L'ANGLAISE

This is what Walter Scott calls venison in his novels. Who is there who has not wanted to eat Walter Scott's venison and Fenimore Cooper's bison's hump?

Unfortunately, bisons live at a considerable distance from us. The same is not true of the deer which we have in all our forests; but it is true that these are reserved for the royal pleasure, and that our deer are less good than the English ones.

When you have a quarter of deer, wash it in tepid water, wipe it with a cloth, salt it and wrap it in buttered paper. Then enclose it in a large sheet of pastry, made simply with flour and lukewarm water, to the thickness of a centime. Carefully seal the joins, and support the pastry by covering it in turn with buttered paper. Roast the quarter for three hours, basting it every ten minutes. When it is cooked, unwrap it and arrange it on a hot platter. Prick the quarter of deer with the point of a knife in order to have the meat juices run out. Serve immediately, with a sauceboat of currant jelly and with a dish of white beans which have just been drained and buttered.

RICE   *RIZ*

Originally from the Orient, rice ranks immediately after bread as the healthiest, most abundant and most universally known food. The peoples of Asia, Africa and America are big consumers of rice and thrive on it. Rice is much used in many European countries too.

An amber-tinted white wine is also made from rice in some countries and tastes as good as Spanish wine. This inebriating wine is much used in China, where rice forms the basis of the people's diet.

The rice which we eat in France comes from Italy, from Piedmont and from the Carolinas.

Riz à la chancelière (a recipe of la présidente Fouquet) •
Rice in the Lady Chancellor's style

Put the following ingredients in a big earthenware *marmite*, which must be higher than it is wide: half a pound of rice which has been rinsed six times in tepid water, half a pound of powdered sugar, a quarter pound of fresh butter, three spoonfuls of white honey, a small spoonful of finely ground cinnamon and, finally, two *pintes* (a little less than two litres) of very fresh milk. Put the *marmite* in the bread oven at the same time as the bread and let the rice cook until the time comes for your big twelve-pound loaf to be taken out.

Take good note that the *marmite*, which must be of a good height, should be more or less empty in its upper part, so that the milk, when made to boil by the great heat of the oven, cannot escape from the pipkin and is obliged to keep falling back on the rice.

Madame la chancelière de Pontchartrain has lived for a long time on this food, which is both agreeable and light and which is very salubrious for inflammations of the chest and stomach.

ROQUEFORT   *ROQUEFORT (fromage de)*

A cheese which is made at Roquefort-en-Rouergue in Aveyron.

This cheese is made of a mixture of goat's and ewe's milk, heated and put in a mould under pressure. Next, each little mass of cheese is encircled with bands to prevent it from cracking open. It is dried in cellars where there is plenty of movement in the air. The cheeses are then salted. This is done by covering them with a layer of salt and then, after the salting has lasted for three or four days, stacking them on top of each other. They are left for a while to become refined; and care is taken to scrape and clean them whenever a slightly coloured bloom appears. As soon as this bloom is red and white, these cheeses are good to eat. This is usually after three or four months in the cellar.

We recommend Roquefort cheese, which is considered with good reason to be the best of all our dry cheeses.

SAMPHIRE   *BACILE*

This is a plant which belongs to the umbelliferous species. It grows on the sea shore, amongst the rocks. I have picked it on all the shores of Normandy. The stems are tough, green and embellished with fleshy leaves. The folioles are narrow, the flowers white, with a salty, piquant and aromatic flavour, but for all that still very agreeable. The stems are preserved in vinegar and are eaten like gherkins and Indian pickles.

SEA URCHIN   *OURSIN*

A round shellfish, which is also called *châtaigne de mer* (sea chestnut), since its appearance is exactly like that of a chestnut still enclosed in its prickly shell. Its prickles serve it as feet and, when they become worn down, the animal rolls along like a billiard ball.

When you open this crustacean [echinoderm would

be the correct expression, since the sea urchin belongs to a class of creature quite separate from the crustaceans] you find a little red animal, of a salty flavour, who is the owner of the house. Its eggs, which are dark yellow, are attached to the interior walls of the shell. Those who are not disgusted by this sort of living purée eat them as they would an egg, with sippets.

The best sea urchins are those of the Mediterranean. They anticipate storms and withstand them by attaching themselves to the strongest marine plants. They excrete by means of the tiny vents, of which more than twelve thousand have been counted, in their spines.

STEWS   *RAGOÛTS*

Stews, above all, were responsible for the brilliance of old French cookery; yet it is stews which bring disgrace on contemporary cuisines, especially that of England.

Never will a cuisine other than our own attain the heights reached by our piquant sauces, or the delicacy of our *blanquettes* or our *poulettes*.

In the same way, you can take a trip around the world, and you will not find a cook, be he cordon rouge or cordon bleu, who can make you an omelette as good as that made by the mother of a family for her husband's and children's dinner.

First of all, a word about the *salpicons*.

These fillings are made with all sorts of meats and vegetables, such as sweetbreads, truffles, mushrooms, artichoke hearts, etc. But if they are to be good, the meats and vegetables used (which should be in equal proportions) must be cooked separately. In this way they can all be cooked to the same extent, according to their nature.

Salpicon ordinaire • An ordinary *salpicon*

This is made of veal sweetbreads, *foie-gras*, or *demi-gras*, ham, mushrooms and truffles, if they are in season. Dice these into small cubes of the same size. Have ready an espagnole sauce which has been considerably reduced; the quantity to be sufficient for your meat and vegetables. When you are ready, put it all on the stove, stir it without allowing it to boil, and then serve.

One makes this filling in the same way for *quenelles* (forcemeat balls) or a *godiveau* (forcemeat pie) or when using the white meat of spit-roasted poultry, cocks' combs or artichoke hearts. It depends on what is available and what is the season.

Ragoût de céleri • Celery stew (Recipe of Dr Rocques)

Cook some chopped celery and endive and spinach. Season with pepper, salt and nutmeg, moisten with some good bouillon and serve with golden croûtons. If you are rather partial to them, you can even put a few ortolans or a few fillets of red partridge on this delicate bed. Taste this dish, dear companions in gourmandise, and perhaps you will be satisfied with it.

Ragoût de haricots à la bretonne •

Stewed haricot beans as they are prepared in Britanny Take some beans from Soissons; it doesn't matter whether they are fresh or dried. Pick them over, and wash a litre of them. Put them in a *marmite* with cold water and a piece of unsalted butter. Heat, adding a little cold water from time to time, which will halt the boiling and make the beans softer. When they are cooked, drain them, and put them in a casserole with a bit of butter, one or two spoonfuls of puréed onions in a brown sauce and some espagnole sauce. Season with coarsely ground pepper and salt, sauté them frequently, and finish them with a pat of butter.

TOMATOES   *TOMATES*

A fruit which comes to us from the people of the south, who treat it with honour. Its flesh is eaten in purée form and its sweet juice is used as a seasoning.

TRUFFLE   *TRUFFE*

Here we have come to the gastronomes' holy of holies (the *sacrum sacrorum*); to the word which gourmands throughout the ages have never pronounced without lifting their hands to their hats; to the *tuber cibarium*, to the *lycoperdon gulosorum*, to the truffle.

You have questioned scholars, asking them exactly what this tubercle is, and after two thousand years of discussion the scholars reply as they did on the first day: 'We don't know.' You have interrogated the truffle itself, and the truffle has replied to you: 'Eat me and adore God.' To recount the history of the truffle would be to take on the task of relating the history of world civilization. Silent though they are, they have played a greater role in this than the laws of Minos, than the tables of Solon; and they have done so during all the great periods of the nations and throughout the shining hours of the mighty empires. They abounded in Rome, Greece and Libya. The Barbars, coming on them, trampled them underfoot and caused them to disappear. From the time of Augustulus until Louis XV they effaced themselves. They reappeared only in the eighteenth century; and reached their zenith under the parliamentary government between 1820 and 1848.

The *Dictionnaire de la Conversation* states that in France there are several types of truffles; black, grey, violet and garlic-scented. They are gathered in many of our *départements*. The limestone chain which runs through the *départements* of Aube, Haute-Marne and the Côte-d'Or provides the grey truffle which is almost as delicate as the white garlic-scented truffle from Piedmont. The black truffle abounds in Perigord, Angoumois and Quercy. It is also to be found in Gard, Drôme, Isère, Vaucluse, Hérault, Tarn, the eastern Pyrénées and in the Jura mountains, Ardèche and Lozère. Several forests in Touraine produce truffles of good quality.

Brillat-Savarin says that the truffle is the diamond of the kitchen; that it awakens erotic and gourmand memories in the skirted sex, and gourmand and erotic souvenirs in the bearded sex. The truffle is certainly not a positive aphrodisiac, but in certain circumstances it can make women more tender, and men more amiable.

About truffles in general
The truffle holds the first place among the cryptogams: the orange agaric, that mushroom of kings, *Fungus Caesareus*, as it was called by our old botanists, has only second place.

Rather than being indigestible, as has been said repeatedly, the truffle promotes the functions of the stomach (providing that it is used with restraint), and owes its digestive properties to its mildly stimulating molecules. It is nourishing, restoring, warming to cold temperaments. Meats, vegetables, fish and other food-stuffs, whatever they may be, become lighter if they are flavoured with truffles. Nevertheless, there have been some authors whose palates have never been able to savour these delicious tubercles, and who have reproached them for troubling the digestion, causing insomnia and producing a disposition to apoplexy and to nervous diseases. We have consulted a fair number of truffle devotees, some old, others young. They all unan-imously acclaim its beneficent action. One of them, a very witty middle-aged man, and of an amiable nature such as all true gastronomes possess, said to me a few days ago:

'When I eat truffles, I become livelier, gayer and more alert; I feel internally, especially in my veins, a sweet and voluptuous warmth, which is not slow to communicate itself to my brain. My ideas are clearer and simpler. If it suits me, I compose verses on the spot for rich poets, I compose speeches for worried savants or for lazy dep-uties, and then I fall asleep. My digestion works easily, my sleep is untroubled. What is said about certain vir-tues of the truffle is ancient history for me.'

Besides, who does not know the truffle and its incom-parable aroma? Is there a natural product which is more famous amongst ancient and modern peoples? The Romans liked it passionately, and demanded it from Africa.

'Libyan,' exclaimed Juvenal, 'unyolk your cattle, keep your harvests, but send us your truffles.'

I belong to the era when truffles have been most in fashion. The Bourbons of the older branch were said to govern with truffles. There were two queens of the stage who particularly acknowledged the influence of these estimable tubercles; Mlle Georges and Mlle Mars.

Every evening when these ladies were acting, and particularly during the period of their greatest successes, supper was available at their homes for some of their intimate friends. They returned to their dwelling with the courtiers from the boxes and found at home the courtiers of the house.

At the house of Georges, truffles were always eaten in the same way.

At the house of Mars, it was up to the cook, and he had carte blanche in this matter.

But at the house of Agrippine [i.e. Mlle Georges], she who embodied every form of sensuality, no mercy was shown to the truffle, it was compelled to yield every sensation which it was capable of giving.

Hardly had she arrived home when perfumed water in a shallow basin of the most beautiful porcelain was brought to Georges, in which she washed her hands. Then the truffles were brought, truffles which had already been subjected to two or three ablutions and the same number of scrubbings; and, in a separate plate, a little vermilion fork and a little knife with a mother-of-pearl handle and a steel blade.

Then Agrippine, with her hand modelled on classical lines, with her fingers of marble and her rosy fingernails, started to peel the black tubercle, an ornament in her hand, in the most adroit fashion in the world. She cut it in thin tiny leaves like paper, poured on some ordinary pepper and a few atoms of Cayenne pepper, impregnated them with white oil from Lucca or green oil from Aix, and then passed the salad bowl to a servant, who tossed the salad which she had prepared.

The rest of the supper, depending on the season, consisted of a roast of game, a chicken from Bresse or from Mans, or a fine turkey from Bourges.

And then came the salad, for which the supper had only been a prologue. It is difficult to imagine the scent which the truffle attained, seasoned merely with oil and pepper.

One scooped out by the forkful from this salad bowl, as one might have from an ordinary salad.

At Mlle Mars, the service was much more complicated, but the salad lacked, in point of dressing, the beautiful hands, the pink fingernails and, more than anything, the abandon and the charming permissiveness of Agrippine.

The most ancient recipe for truffles which we can offer to our readers is that of Apicius.

Ragoût de truffes à l'Apicius
First cook your truffles in water, then put them on a skewer, and let them turn five or six times over a fire. Baste them with oil, lemon juice, chervil, pepper and salt. When the sauce boils, bind it with eggs and wine.

[This recipe does not correspond, except in a very general way, to any of the six given by Apicius (VII, xiv). The first of these, given below, may be what Dumas had in mind:

'*Truffles.* Peel the truffles, cook them in water, powder them with salt, impale them on skewers and grill them over a gentle heat. Next, put in an earthenware *marmite* some olive oil, garum (a kind of fish sauce), sweet wine which has been reduced, ordinary wine, pepper and honey. Bring this to the boil, then bind it with (some form of) starch. Take the truffles off their skewers and serve them (with the sauce).']

Salade aux truffes à la toulousaine •

A truffle salad from Toulouse M. Urbain Dubois, an outstanding French cook who practises abroad, gives us the following recipe and accompanying eulogy:

'This dish is a recent creation of Toulousaine science and proves that in France the great art of gastronomy is practised everywhere with equal earnestness and always with success.

'Choose five or six fresh black truffles with a good aroma, and three tender artichokes. Carefully brush the truffles, then wash, peel and chop them up very finely and put them in a closed container. Trim away the tough leaves of the artichokes, leaving only those which are unquestionably tender. Divide them through the middle and lengthwise, slice them as thinly as the truffles and let them macerate with a little salt for ten minutes; then wipe them on a cloth.

'Sieve the yolks of three hardboiled eggs, put them in a terrine, add a little mustard and dilute with half a glass of finest quality oil and a little good tarragon vinegar. Rub the bottom of a salad bowl with garlic, and arrange the artichokes and truffles alternately in layers in this. Season with salt and pepper as well as with a part of the eggs which have been mixed with oil. Ten minutes later toss the truffles and the artichokes in the salad bowl, to blend the seasoning. This salad is worthy of bearing a great name.'

TURMERIC (or CURCUMA)
TERRA MERITA ou CURCUMA

This is an oriental root which, like saffron, gives a yellow colour which is used for colouring ragoûts.

Turmeric is one element in curry powder, which is used extensively in India and which is employed in certain dishes in Europe.

Curry powder is made with 120 grams of hot red pepper, 90 grams of turmeric, 30 grams of pepper, 30 grams of cloves and a little nutmeg, all ground to a fine powder.

The English add rhubarb to this. It is well known that one of the gastronomic diversions of the English is to eat little rhubarb tarts and little rhubarb pies. This fashion has been introduced by the English to the pastry-makers of the quarter Saint-Honoré in Paris.

TURNIP   *NAVET*

Vegetables themselves have their own aristocracy and privileges. It is accepted that the three best kinds of turnip which can be grown are those from Cressy, from Belle-Isle-en-Mer and from Meaux. But, whether this results from intrigue or ingenuity, the turnips with which Paris is currently supplied come from Freneuse and Vaugirard.

The first recipe which comes to hand is entitled *Navets à la d'Esclignac*. What can possibly have earned M. d'Esclignac the honour of giving his name to a dish of turnips? In this field, there is no odder subject of study than the books written by cooks and the strange way in which they suddenly make up their minds to make a sauce of, to put on the grill, or to roast our famous men.

This is what we find in one single book, in the section on soups:

Potage à la Demidoff.	Potage au mont Blanc.
– à la John Russell.	– à la Magenta et à la
– à l'Abd-el-Kader.	Solferino.
– à la ville de Berlin.	– aux Dardanelles.
– à la Cialdini.	– à la Dumas.
– au 15 septembre 1864.	– à la Thérésa.
– au héros de Palestro.	– à la mère l'Oie.
– à la Lucullus.	– à la Rothschild.
– à la Guillaume Tell.	

If we then carry on from soup to hors d'oeuvre, we find the following, the reasons for which again escape us:

Petits soufflés au Caire.	– à la Louisiane.
Petits pâtés à la Turbigo.	– à la Capodimonte.
Petits pâtés Inkermann.	– à l'Africaine.
Filets de merlans à la	Friture au nouveau monde.
Durando.	– à la fleuriste Florentine.
Petites timbales à la	Petites timbales à la Titus.
Garibaldi.	Soufflés à la Marc Aurèle.
Friture au prince impérial.	Pâtés Omer-Pacha.

Petites bouchées aux vrais amis.	Petits soufflés à la Cellini.
Bâtons à la Palmerston.	Petits soufflés au désir.

[Dumas also gives amusing examples of titles for *relevés*, *entrées chaudes*, *entrées froides* and *rôts*.]

We could carry on giving further lists from this historic writer on cooking, who is at the same time an excellent cook. But in quoting him, it need hardly be said, we will not deprive ourselves of the right to borrow some of his strangely titled recipes.

Let us return to our turnips.

Navets glacés au jus • Turnips with a meat glaze

Choose clean turnips of equal size, suitable to be cut into shapes like pears. Blanch and drain them, and butter the bottom of a casserole which is the right size to take them side by side. Arrange the turnips in this and cook them until golden-brown in butter and sugar. Moisten them with excellent bouillon, and sprinkle over them sugar, a few grains of salt and some bits of cinnamon stick. Bring to the boil on a high heat, cover with a piece of buttered paper, and put at the side of the oven with a flame below. Put the lid on the casserole, and hot embers on the lid. Once the turnips are cooked, uncover them, glaze them, arrange them on a platter, pour a little good bouillon into the casserole to dislodge the pan juices, remove the cinnamon sticks, and pour the sauce over the turnips as you would for a compote.

I notice that I have unfairly skipped over turnips *à la d'Esclignac*, the recipe which was the reason for the lengthy parenthesis from which we have just emerged. I make haste to redress the injustice.

Navets à la d'Esclignac

Take some turnips four or five inches long and cut off their two ends. Split each in two and then, in peeling the halves, shape each like a rope; this is done by using the end of a knife to fashion two little grooves such as one finds on rope.

Blanch the prepared turnips and put them in a casserole in the same manner as in the preceding recipe. Season and cook them in the same way, but do not add any cinnamon. Once they have finished cooking, put a little espagnole in the casserole to help dislodge the pan juices, add a little butter and pour the sauce over the turnips.

VANILLA   *VANILLE (Epidendrum vanilla)*

An exotic plant belonging to the orchid family. It always grows in the shade, either in the crannies of rocks or at the foot of huge trees. The aroma of vanilla is very delicate and has such perfect fragrance that it is used to flavour creams, liqueurs and chocolates.

VIOLET   *VIOLETTE*

This is a flower whose very name evokes numerous thoughts of Spring. Whoever speaks of the violet speaks of shade, of freshness, of modesty, of a stream running through grass. There is not a poet, whether an erotic like Parny or a romantic such as Hugo, who has not found the word violet at the end of his rhyme; it is a gentle and fragrant name. The cornflour, charming sapphire of the wheat fields, comes after the violet in the poetical ranking of wild flowers. Alive, it is destined to adorn the bodices of young maidens; dead, it lends its fragrance to confectionery, liqueurs, sherbets, preserves, and other household culinary preparations.

Violet ice cream is a dainty dish, among the most esteemed of all delicacies.

Sirope de Violettes • Syrup of violets

Is there any old person, whatever his age and however close to the grave he may be, who does not see at the other extreme of his life his mother approaching his cradle with a steaming cup in her hand and bringing a perfumed liquid to his lips? This perfumed liquid was syrup of violets.

Pick half a pound of violet flowers (those from the woods are the best) and put them in a terrine or other container which can be stopped up. Boil three half *setiers* (¾ litre) of water, but leave this for ten minutes after you have taken it from the fire before you pour it on the violets, because the infusion, which ought to be of a beautiful violet colour, would become green if the water was too close to the boil. Put the infusion into a drying oven (*à l'étuve*) so that it stays hot until the next day, at which point you take out the flowers, and press them well in a napkin in order to extract the dye. Put this in a terrine with three pounds of powdered sugar, which you then melt. Put the terrine back into the drying oven for a further twenty-four hours, stirring from time to time.

Keep the drying oven hot during all this time, as you would for sugar-candy. This produces two bottles of syrup; you must be careful before putting it in the bottles to boil it to the pearl stage, so that the syrup will keep properly and not ferment.

Of all the syrups this is the only one which is made without cooking.

WATER   *EAU*

People who habitually drink water become just as good gourmets about water as wine drinkers about wine.

For fifty or sixty years of my life, I have drunk only water, and no lover of wine has ever felt the same delight in some Grand-Laffite or Chambertin as I have in a glass of cool spring water whose purity has not been tainted by any earthy salts.

Very cold water, even when it has been artificially cooled with ice, acts as an excellent tonic to the stomach, without provoking any irritation and indeed calming any which might already have existed.

But this is not the case with water coming from melted snow or ice, which are heavy because they contain no air. Stir these waters well before drinking, and they will lose their injurious qualities.

Formerly all of Paris slaked its thirst from the river which traverses it. Nowadays the water comes from Grenelle; pipes bring it to the mountain of Sainte-Geneviève, whence it is distributed throughout Paris. For the last five or six years, water from the Dhuys has been competing with this; it comes from the other side, that is to say from Belleville, Montmartre and the Buttes Chaumont.

The water from the Seine was the object of so many calumnies for such a long time, particularly by people from the provinces coming to pass a few days in Paris, that it grew weary of slaking the thirst of two million ungrateful persons. But when the waters of the Seine were well purified and when it was drawn from above the zoological gardens, and from the middle of the stream, no other water was comparable to it for limpidity, lightness and sapidity. Above all, it was abundantly saturated with oxygen, having been turned over and over by the multiple meanderings which, over a distance of nearly two hundred leagues (eight hundred kilometres), subjected it to the action of the atmosphere's air. Moreover, it flows along a bed of sand all the way from its source until it reaches Paris. Gourmands attribute to this circumstance the superior quality of fish from the Seine to those from other rivers.

Everyone knows that monks have never really liked water very much; here is one more incident which proves their antipathy for this 'dreary liquid'. A Franciscan friar used to visit a bishop's kitchen fairly assiduously, the latter having told his people to look after the good brother. One day, when the prelate was holding a big dinner, the monk happened to be at the bishopric. The monseigneur was talking about the holy man, and recommending him to the assembled company. Right away, several of the ladies exclaimed:

'Monseigneur, you must amuse us by playing a trick on the monk. Summon him, and we will give him a beautiful glass of clear water which we will present to him as a glass of excellent white wine.'

'But you're not seriously thinking of such a thing, ladies!' said the bishop.

'Oh, but it would amuse us, let us do it, Monseigneur.'

So they summoned a manservant, and had him prepare a bottle of water on the spot. This was fastened up properly, and correctly labelled. Then they had the mendicant friar summoned.

'Brother,' said the ladies, 'you must drink to the health of his Grace and to ours.'

The monk was congratulating himself on his good fortune, and prepared himself to receive it well. The bottle was uncorked and a bumper drink was poured out. However, the crafty monk, who immediately saw through the deceit, did not lose his head at all, and said in the most woeful and humble tone to the bishop: 'Monseigneur, I will not drink as you have not given your holy blessing to this nectar.'

'This is quite unnecessary, my brother.'

'But in the name of all the saints of Paradise, I implore you to do so, Monseigneur.'

The ladies joined in the discussion, and implored the prelate to have the good nature to do this for them. The bishop finally bowed to their wishes, and blessed the water. The Franciscan then called a lackey and said to him, smiling: 'Champagne, take that into the church, a Franciscan has never drunk holy water.'

He was really quite right, wasn't he?

WHITEBAIT   *WHITE-BAIT*

Whitebait, a name meaning white fish, is undoubtedly one of the most popular dishes of London.

I recall having been invited, just in the ordinary way and without any special reason, by one of my friends who was back from Indre to go and eat whitebait at Greenwich [spelled *Grennisch* in the French text]. I found the invitation so unusual that I went there at once.

The whitebait is a tiny fish which is called *yanchette* in Italy, *pontin* at Nice and, quite simply, *poisson blanc* at Bordeaux. [This statement is broadly true, in that whitebait are the fry of various clupeoid, i.e. herring-like, fish; and so are the tiny fish sold as *bianchetti* in Italy and as *poutinou* at Nice. But in Britain whitebait are the fry of herring and sprats, whereas the Mediterranean counterpart of whitebait is a mixture of the fry of anchovies and sardines.]

On this occasion the whitebait were the crowning feature of a dinner of three services [each service comprising several different dishes], all of fish. I was curious to see how they prepared this dish, to eat which people would come from two or three hundred leagues away [550 to 800 miles – the meaning is, in effect, from all over England and Wales and parts of Scotland]. Handfuls of the fish were washed in iced water, then laid out on a cloth to drain. They were kept on the cloth, over ice, for twenty minutes. When the time came to serve them, they were rolled in fresh breadcrumbs and then placed in a napkin with a handful of flour. The cook took the napkin by both ends, squeezing it and shaking it in such a way as to propel the fish, in a single avalanche, into a metal sieve so fine that only the flour could pass through it. He shook the sieve and then plunged it, with the fish in it, into very hot frying oil. One minute of cooking was enough. As soon as the fish had taken on a good colour, they were removed from the sieve, dusted with salt and a little cayenne, arranged *en buisson* [in a pyramid – the term is normally used for an arrangement of shrimps or prawns in this fashion] on a folded napkin and served at once. [The description is recognizable, but the rolling in fresh breadcrumbs is unusual and indeed hardly seems possible with such small fish. The reference to handfuls of the fish should not be taken as meaning that they were picked up in handfuls. Great care was taken to avoid handling them.]

YOUNG WILD BOAR   *MARCASSIN*

The young wild boar goes by the name of *bête rousse* in hunting terms. It is excellent with any of the sauces normally served with fully grown boar, that is to say spit-roasted or grilled with onions. In olden times young wild boar were not eaten at all, but were castrated and then released in the forest. Thus brought to perfection – and this is the term used of the singers in the Sistine chapel – they become fatter, more delicate, and less wild.

Quartier de marcassin, sauce aux cerises •

Quarter of wild boar with cherry sauce

Choose a fresh tender quarter of young wild boar, without rind. Remove the bone from the chump end and break with a straight cut and bend back the bone protruding at the other end. Salt the quarter and put it in a terrine with a litre of marinade which has been cooked and is now half-cool. Let the quarter macerate for two or three days, then drain it, sponge it off on a cloth and put it in a shallow baking tin with some lard. Cover it with greased paper and cook it for three quarters of an hour, basting it frequently with the fat. Then add a few spoonfuls of the marinade, and cook for an additional half hour, continuing to baste the meat with the pan juices.

When the meat is well 'seized', remove the baking tin from the oven, drain the meat and mask it with a thick layer of grated breadcrumbs (from black bread) which have been dried, pounded, sieved, mixed with a little sugar and cinnamon, and then dampened with some good red wine, but only enough to make them stick together. Over this layer sprinkle breadcrumbs which have not been moistened. Baste the meat with the fat from the baking tin, put it back on this, and keep it at the front of the oven for a half an hour. When you are about to serve it, take it out of the oven, put a paper frill around the protruding bone, arrange it on a platter and serve the following sauce in a separate vessel.

Sauce aux cerises • Cherry sauce
[In a little water] soften two handfuls of dry black cherries, such as are commonly sold in Germany, that is to say with the stones in. Next, pound them in a mortar, then add a glass of red wine to thin them, and pour the mixture into a vessel which must not be tinned. Add a piece of cinnamon, two cloves, a grain of salt and a piece

of lemon zest. Boil the liquid for two minutes, and thicken it with a little starch diluted with water. Put the vessel on the side of the fire, cover it, keep it thus for a quarter of an hour and then strain the sauce.

(Recipe of M. Urbain Dubois, cook to Their Royal Majesties of Prussia.)

ZEST   *ZESTE*

This is what the yellow epidermis of the skin of a lemon is called. The name applies also to oranges and citrons.

Zest is removed in thin slices. The essential oils which give the fruits of this family their aroma are present especially in the zest. The white matter which lies underneath the zest is completely lacking in these, and also has a rather disagreeable bitterness; it is for this reason that it is recommended always to separate the two with care.

GREAT FOOD

BUFFALO CAKE AND INDIAN PUDDING

Dr A. W. Chase

TRAVELLING PHYSICIAN, SALESMAN, author and self-made man, Dr Chase dispensed remedies all over America during the late nineteenth century, collecting recipes and domestic tips from the people he met along the way. His self-published books became celebrated US bestsellers and were the household bibles of their day.

Containing recipes for American-style treats, such as Boston cream cakes, Kentucky corn dodgers and pumpkin pie, as well as genial advice on baking bread and testing whether a cake is cooked, this is a treasure trove of culinary wisdom from the homesteads of a still rural, pioneering United States.

GREAT FOOD

THE CAMPAIGN FOR DOMESTIC HAPPINESS

Isabella Beeton

FIRMLY OF THE BELIEF THAT A HOME should
be run as an efficient military campaign, Mrs Beeton,
the doyenne of English cookery, offers timeless tips
on selecting cuts of meat, throwing a grand party
and hosting a dinner, as well as giving suggestions
on staff wages and the cost of each recipe.

With such delicious English classics as rabbit pie,
carrot soup, baked apple custard, and fresh lemonade
– as well as invalid's jelly for those days when stewed
eels may be a little too much – this is a wonderful
collection of food writing from the matriarch
of modern housekeeping.

'Sublime . . . A Victorian gem'
JULIAN BARNES

GREAT FOOD

EXCITING FOOD FOR
SOUTHERN TYPES

Pellegrino Artusi

PELLEGRINO ARTUSI is the original icon of
Italian cookery, whose legendary 1891 book *Science
in the Kitchen and the Art of Eating Well* defined its
national cuisine and is still a bestseller today.

He was also a passionate gastronome, renowned
host and brilliant raconteur, who filled his books with
tasty recipes and rumbustious anecdotes. From an
unfortunate incident regarding minestrone in Livorno
and a proud defence of the humble meat loaf, to
digressions on the unusual history of ice-cream, the
side-effects of cabbage and the Florentines' weak
constitutions, these writings brim with gossip, good
cheer and an inexhaustible zest for life.

'The fountainhead of modern Italian cookery'
GASTRONOMICA